Poetry of Transition: Mexican Poetry of the 1960s and 1970s

Edited by
Linda Scheer & Miguel Florez Ramirez

Translation Press

ACKNOWLEDGEMENTS

Several of the translations have appeared in the following periodicals and books in the U.S.: *Chelsea, Paintbrush, Poetry Now, Black Warrior Review, Footprint, kayak, The Nation, Partisan Review, The Whale's Scars* (New Rivers Press) and *The Day of Vendors* (Calavera Press). We also wish to thank the following publishing houses in Mexico: Editorial Era, Universidad Nacional Autónoma de México, Fondo de Cultura Económica, Editorial Joaquín Mortiz, siglo veintiuno editores, Imaginaria, Multiarte, La Maquina Electrica Editorial, Cuadernos de Estraza, La Máquina de Escribir, Xilote, Ediciones Punto de Partida de la UNAM, Libros Escogidos, Ediciones del Instituto National de Bellas Artes and Ediciones del Departamento de Difusión Cultural de la UNAM.

Translation Press
2901 Heatherway
Ann Arbor, Michigan 48104

Library of Congress Cataloging in Publication Data

The Poetry of transition.

    Translation of many poems from the Spanish.
    1. Mexican poetry—20th century—Translations into English. 2. English poetry—Translations from Spanish. I. Scheer, Linda. II. Ramirez, Miguel Flores.
PQ7763.E5P6 1984   861   83—18008
ISBN 0-931556-06-6

Cover Photo: "Sucking Birds" by Francisco Toledo

TABLE OF CONTENTS

PREFACE

The editors of poetry anthologies are frequently accused of the crime of partiality, of being partial to certain poets and to certain poems they have produced. We're not looking for a pardon, nor are we sure that such a crime exists.

More than four years have gone by since we conceived of an anthology which would include the most current poetry written by Mexican poets (not necessarily "Mexican" poetry); an anthology which would extend the scope of *Poesía en movimento*[1] — at that time the only collection of poetry to be assembed with a specific intent — using some of its criteria for selection but without merely repeating the same poets with new poems. Faced with material of more than thirty poets, some of whom were still unpublished, the obvious problem was who to include. We never presumed to create an exhaustive anthology of "new talent," although (and this was clear from the beginning) we did indeed want the selection to reveal the innovations of each poet. The risk was imminent: the result might be an incomplete selection or an anthology which, due to its selective method, would be incriminating.

And so we took the risk by starting with a practical prerequisite: that the poets should not be older than forty at the time the anthology was being formed, and that they should have at least one book published. This could be considered arbitrary; we thought it to be relevant because not all young poets write with the vitality and risk that their age implies. Moreover, many "mature" poets abandon their well-tried formulas to risk new avenues of expression. The latter was our qualitative requirement for selection and, of course, it was the most important.

Once our scope was established, we immediately realized the enormous sacrifice we were making, to the point of thinking that all of the best poets had suddenly turned forty-one. The crime was committed.

Unfortunately, we weren't able to include the talented young poets who did fit the age limit because they were unpublished at the time. For them, Herod's scimitar was more than unjust, since we knew that at the time of the anthology's publication, they would no longer find themselves in that situation. But we also realize that only time will have the last word regarding those who, anthologized or not, will live on within the poetic vein. Here we are only tracing the journey of a few; their transit in an infinite historical process. And that is how we came to select the title for the anthology: *Poetry of Transition*.

Octavio Paz states that poetry is trans-historic reality that comes alive in history: the written word. Perhaps when this selection appears, some of the poets will have changed to such an extent that the material included here will have become a bridge; in effect, it will be a bridge, but constructed of the "here and now," since all of the poets are concerned with works that, while in some cases worked within a traditional form, are open to different interpretations which give them an originality that is continually in motion and which refuses to become stagnated.

The heterogeneity of the poets included (I purposely avoid the word "style") makes it difficult to find a common denominator; it would be impossible to show the path that current poetry in Mexico is taking. An infinite number of diverse elements converge on its production: from the poets' view of the world and its people to individual ideas about culture, society, tradition, literary innovation, etc. And even more so when dealing with writers who live in a society in transition like Mexico, where it is foolish to deny the conflict of Prospero and Caliban. In this sense the problems are both old and new. It would be better to go directly to the poets who speak to us from their own concrete social reality as well as from a language that proclaims new forms, new ways of seeing reality. On both counts, literary creation is not beholden to a single meaning or to mere words of narcissistic rhetoric.

It is important to point out that most of the poets were born into a world crisis at the beginning of World War II, and in the crucial year of 1968 they were going through an existential transition as they profoundly reappraised postwar ideas and attitudes. Perhaps this explains Jaime Reyes' dramatic view of reality (it has been said that he is a "torn, chaotic and visceral" poet); or José Emilio Pacheco's tragic vision; or the divided and disperse concepts of José de Jesús Sampedro; or the timeless and premonitory ideas of José Carlos Becerra. What is certain is that the poets respond, explicitly or implicitly, consciously or unconsciously, to the reality they name and about which they write. It has been said that if one looks for a distinctive trait among Mexico's young poets —to parody a verse from Rafael Alberti —it would be that when they write, they seem to be alone. "It isn't so much that the poet looks for solitude, but that he finds it," Rosario Castellanos would add.

This generation of alienated poets started to come into the poetic limelight in the 70s, with the exception of Pacheco and Aridjis who were already well-known in the previous decade. And it is a generation that reflects its time. In one way or another they seek to "translate" the fast and compulsive reality which surrounds them by searching for a poetic reinterpretation of the world and the rhythm of daily life. José Joaquín Blanco (b. 1951), one of the youngest and most talented Mexican literary critics, states that the poetry of the 70s appears like a transitory expression of everyday life, not sublimating reality,but rather showing it in its corruptible, open and ephemeral forms. Contrary to what could be expected, however, the texts we have included show definite scholarly inclinations which are accentuated in some cases and, in others, assimilated.

We have chosen to divide the poets into three groups: the first includes José Carlos Becerra, José Emilio Pacheco, Francisco Hernández and Homero Aridjis, all of whom successfully seek to renew the Spanish language within a well assimilated formal tradition. The next group includes David Huerta, Jaime Reyes, José de Jesús Sampedro and myself. This second group has attempted to break with expressive traditions by using natural linguistic recourses: through subversion of single meanings, the negation of language itself and experimentation. These elements are harbingers of an eventual discovery of "something else," something as yet not entirely definable. In the final group we find Francisco Cervantes, Marco Antonio Campos, Elva Macías (alas! the only woman on this island) and Ernesto Trejo, all of whom respond to the special sound of other times and places; echoes of an incomplete past that seem to travel through time. Finally, and so as not to break with this heterogeneous frame of reference, a team of seven different translators came into contact with the personal language of twelve very different poets. It should be noted that the translators had the opportunity to work with the majority of the poets on a personal level to throw light upon the many enigmas that came up along the way. Besides the well-known problems that confront the translator, the third group of texts presented the special problem of conserving the different tonalities and shades of language which, as in the case of Francisco Cervantes, were converted into an English reminiscent of Renaissance and pre-Renaissance literature. The translators definitely assumed the role of antiheroes in this adventure.

If we had to summarize in a few lines what has been stated above, we would say that *Poetry of Transition* is the purgatory where the poets await a final verdict.

Miguel Flores Ramírez

1. *Poesía en movimento*,Editorial Siglo XXI, Mexico, 1966 (English translation: *New Poetry of Mexico*, edited by Mark Strand: E.P. Dutton, New York, 1970).

11

POETRY OF TRANSITION

JOSE CARLOS BECERRA (1936-1970), Villahermosa, Tabasco.

Becerra studied philosophy and architecture at the Universidad Nacional Autónoma de México, and in 1969 he was the recipient of a Guggenheim Fellowship which enabled him to travel first to New York and later to London, where he spent six months. In 1970 he visited several European countries; as he went from Naples to cross the peninsula and take the boat that would lead him to Greece, he lost control of the car he was driving and was killed. He was thirty-three.

His poetic work is extensive and was collected posthumously in El otoño recorre las islas, due to the efforts of those who furnished material and especially to those who worked arduously gathering his published as well as his unpublished poems.

His poetry is a maelstrom of surprises which abundantly celebrates his life and death. In shaded and hidden signs he rejoices in the influences he assimilated so well: traces of a romanticism that embrace the Nerudian and junglelike earthiness of Pellicer under an exhuberant geography of solar light; echoes of Claudel and tones of Perse whispering under the intellectual light of Villaurrutia, Gorostiza, Paz... all in long poems filled with nostalgia, memory, sensuality, certainty and doubt: mirror and dream celebrations.

His sudden stop and change of lane are surprising — a transition to less discursive poems, short texts that mark an expressive search and transcendental pursuit replete with elements of humor, at times of bitterness and even of sarcasm.

The premonitory sign of his death is also surprising: a reiteration between the lines, an open prediction. The question is posed: was he his own visionary?

The myth is invented by him, as he makes life and death coexist in a written celebration which once again surprises, even with regard to what he did not accomplish due to his untimely death which surprised him, or did it not?

Published work: El otoño recorre las islas (1973) is a collection of Becerra's complete works (1961-1970), edited by José Emilio Pacheco and Gabriel Zaid.

fragment from: SEATED ON A STONE*

I have disappeared from my own creation
and will reemerge the day I break my death glass,
but then the accident can never be, the innocence of gesture;
no, it won't be possible to break that glass unintentionally,
    like a child with a ball
but head-on and with a fist.

translated by Linda Scheer

*This fragment was chosen by Carlos Pellicer as the epitaph for Becerra's tombstone.

THE RULES OF THE GAME

Everyone should enter his own destruction, retouch
      his breath,
cultivate his exceptions to the rule, the mollusks of his sun,
abstain in the most cruel and diaphanous way
because light must break, eternity must drop
      a pebble into that lament.

Remember the childhood of your mother, the childhood of your death;
away from the world and all desire,
made immune by the lizard and the bird confronting each other
      in all of blood's intentions.
You have felt the mask and its forgery:
      the face
in greenhouses of small and useless ceremonies which still move us.

Under the light of a moon that resembles the nakedness of ancient
      words,
listen to this rhythm, this rolling of the waters,
night is moving its dark wheels, these words are its
      meaning,
and I let myself be carried by what I want to say: what
      I ignore
and this is how the word ponders its silence.

Oh casual night of the word,
oh fate where the word returns to its silence and
      silence to the first word
the first snails, the first starfish appear once again in language,
and creatures of fog place their breath in new mirrors.

He who utters the first word shall drop the first glass,
he who strikes violently at his amazement shall see fire
      in his hair,
he who laughs aloud shall be the first to remain silent,
he who wakes before his time shall surprise his bones
      in semaphore with the trees;
and the sea, like a broken symptom, returns once more to
      hear itself in the distance
and in its breathing we hear once more the sound of the door

18

banging in the wind of infinity.

The moon is born over the sea like man's ancient look.

The first lights
go on at port.

translated by Linda Scheer

RAGTIME

To speak, perhaps to speak at dawn's devouring, in the cold ash,
    in the evidence forever unseen;
to speak in the same space of voice that never reached these words,
    lost in the sound of words like these,
to speak where all we hide is breathing,
crimes committed for us by those of another history,
    the other history that belongs to us.

Dawn won't deny what frays her love,
face to face with the hyena's laugh, the death-bed unbound,
the mousetrap where the royal hopefuls place their anguish like a
    piece of cheese.
This is my part in the feast of dust,
in this flame where I burn my fingers in the transcription, doubting
    what I say,
I tremble so as not to drown in the lethargy of words
    rising to my neck.

This is my part, this is my part in the struggle to pry ourselves
    from death,
to drink the water of other times, of other histories where leisure
    is well intentioned.
This is my part, now that the city makes is sewage speak,
a quiet, a gloomy animal lies in my soul.

Speak of me: I want to learn to speak of you.
Every word to reach my lips will open the door to a dust-covered
    phrase,
a muddy-booted messenger will come in from the road to sit down
    and watch me;
every word to reach my lips carries the darkened message
of that foreshadowed and unknown Word for which I continue to wait.

And now I am drifting in the water of all I say, obliged to a gentle
    whirlpool spinning,
the rhythm of fate pays what my lips may owe, sounds diminish where
    they should be standing,
phantoms   cross the patio in silence.
But what is this foam that covers my face?

But what is this foam that gingerly covers my points of view?
What clay depresses my tongue like dead history in the doorway
of its own verdict?

The way of the rivers is our way of staring,
of binding ourselves for a moment together, by our faces, by our
      love, by our names,
with hands more shallow than the ocean.
And yet, we knew it all the time;
the sea opens its windows so the drowned can see,
so many familiar faces crowd inside the frames,
struggling to see us, to send us their breath,
for the night's invention is no longer in the hands of the gods,
but in the joining of the hands of the living and the dead.

And our phantoms have already been seated, they are waiting in the
      wide halls of autumn,
the night is raising its sails, and a foreigner on the bridge
perverts our mothers and our wives and our maidens while forcing
      them to laugh.

Blood smells like blood, and the wind doesn't pass by the same
      tree twice,
the city lights blossom like an infant's wound,
swamp-ash is pure gold.

And the drunkard trips on the silent and darkened street, he
      splits the scribe's memory in two;
his hand staggers in the light of the drying blood,
      the exclamation is dissolved in its points of suspension,
what was named becomes darker where words break from what is
      only good for language;
and his stumbling splits the song in two—the song of the woman
      combing her soul before she goes to the solitary bed,
and it splits the hours of the night like a glass that falls from
      the hand of a frightened child.

It splits the city in two, in two the words where memory and
      deed briefly exchange,
in two the word, and so divided, reflects itself,
in two the lovers' struggle for their skin, for each other, and

perhaps they will meet in the interruption.
It splits in two what was already divided, what couldn't be
      touched because we forgot its name, its self-devotion.
It splits the city in two, in two the stumbling of another drunk
      on the silent and darkened street,
and an empty tram, with lights ablaze, stops by our side at the
      corner,
and with gestures we well understand, the conductor demands we
      deliver our dead, for only he is the one to guide them.

But yet there is something, something in the mud, and something in
      the stare of the man who tortures his tongue describing death,
and yet there is something, something in the mud and the word of the
      man who has heard the vacuum slam its doors,
there's something sweet and stubborn in the dark saline stains
      that dawn leaves on the face of the port's new comers,
there's something in the camphor where the old clothes
      invisibly rot,
without organic ostentation, without bloody combat;
there's something that goes to memory and beyond, something that
      stands in front of us.
It doesn't matter if tears unveil their miniscule teeth, that
      feeble nip on the cheeks is a slap on the soul;
so we lower our heads, we'd like to stop, we'd like to lower our
      voices to the depths of an empty well,
and there's a blinking of cities, a visceral movement in the energy
      of those who awaken with their dreams undeciphered.

The night is tossing its crowns to the sea,
and the city, resting on its walls, sitting in the dust,
the city will dictate its words to the scribe, and the stumbling
      of a drunkard on a silent and darkened street
will split its words in two.

And now you will listen to the rat-eaten laws,
you will listen to the rats consuming bookshelves and government
      signatures,
and you will listen as well to the voyage of the sleepers
      through their forgotten waters.

Tomorrow I shall speak the word that will dawn the next day
                       in puddles.

Tomorrow I shall speak the word, the warrior
in this banquet of winter animals.

translated by Sandro Cohen

LA VENTA

In Tabasco, almost at the mouth of the Tonalá river, there is a place called La Venta, where the remains of altars and the mammouth heads of an ancient Olmec culture were found.

It is strange that in such a terribly inhospitable place—a kind of island surrounded by a swamp—these monumental remains of basaltic rock have been found. The way in which these monolithic tons of basalt were transported from the counterforts of the southern Sierra Madre—places where this rock is produced and which did indeed offer magnificent living conditions—through jungles and swamps, and the reason they were carved and erected in such a strange place remain an enigma.

> I have heard
> Laughter in the noises of beasts that make strange noises.
>
> T.S. Eliot

I

It was night when the sea disappeared from the faces of the
    castaways like a sacred expression.
It was night when the foam took leave of the land like a
    word as yet unspoken.
It was night
and the land was the greatest castaway among all those men,
among all, the land was
like the waters' device.

And now, in the places not yet determined by reason,
in the inner square of the Public Plaza,
the breeze seems to engender that distant smell
of animals and prisoners wounded beneath the arrows or ready with
    the lance
or led to the presence of the hand that orders and signals,
    buoyed by its rings and bracelets,
from the basic places of power: necessity and crime.

Where are the men who gave this battle-cry and
    this dream-cry?
Where are those who led the word
and were taken by it to the place of prayer and to the mass of
    silence?

Hunger wavers between the stone and the hand that will
    build its soul's suspicion;
sombre inhabitant silent beneath your works, lead me to the
    scattered hymn that floats ashen among the rotting
    leaves.
Anoint each word of mine with each silence of yours,
        but let not the spark of his mutual language blind us,
so that the dead shall look out among the burning coals of
    what is said
and the phrase shall bend with the weight of time.

                            IV

Night opens like a great book over the sea.
Tonight
the waves softly brush their backs against the beach
like a herd of animals still pure.

Night opens like a great illegible book over the jungle.
The dead walk scattered in the living,
the living dream holding their temples in the dead
and sleep infects its images with stone.

Night opens over you, stone heads that sleep
        like a warning.

The moon pauses over the marshland,
monkeys moan.

There, in the distance, the sea wanders about in its exile,
        awaiting the hour
of its invincible task.

                                December, 1964—November, 1965

                                translated by Linda Scheer

25

THE MALTESE FALCON (for Carlos Monsivais)

Today, with nothing but your picture to keep you afloat,
you are down to ways of disappearing from yourself, down to
     effacing yourself from what you wanted;
the moss that sprouts over your resurrection is the moss
     growing on your body, your invisible body trapped in a
     sharp photo, and everything
you thought you loved or which you simply hated offhandedly
once more glistens outside of you in the cornerstone of another
     chill,
while someone who exits through the door of your picture,
     feels how the night is a sheet drawn over your death
     in a basement bar of some old building along Third Avenue
and somewhere else lights go on,
the spotlights that picked you out
or gathered the shadows of your grimace—deliberate descent to hell—
where the smell of gunpowder would haze over the outline emerging
     from the mirror
into which you would fire your gun.

So, you were re-composing the scene around you,
with the sober eyes that an alcoholic uses
to track down the noose of his terror,
making use, even, of the dust laid over your eyes by the fist blows
and by the perplexed dampness of love;
a glass of scotch in the heart of your secret,
the night's journey recreated on your face by one of the spotlights,
the cold mouth of a .38 automatic ribbed against your stomach
     while the mouth of nothingness seemed to nibble at it,
and the long-legged woman with high cheek bones and a voice fresh
     out of lovemaking or cigarettes,
watching you from a dark corner of the bar,
and all the while it was in her body that the Infinite untangled
     the maze
that at times replaces the act of pulling the trigger.

Oh yes, everything that you coveted;
what you allowed your face to conjure up,
before which your fists and your gun went free, where your grimace
     and your smile forever blended,

delighted, each obsessed with the other, your two insane servants.
So, nothing was left of all that
nor of the office with the view of the skyscrapers
        and the San Francisco wharf among them.

It was you, with the whims of a defeated fighter, your derisive look,
it was the secret places where you went on healing your wounds,
any one of the scenes where you were on the verge of slamming the
        door behind you, blotting out everything;
with face mangled by blows and kicks,
you too searching for the *Maltese Falcon* in which you never believed,
because, maybe in order to find it, believing was a bad omen,
or perhaps because hope would have brought you sooner to defeat
which, in spite of everything, you never expected.

Gone, all those women
encased in their silk stockings,
encased in their circles of flesh frothing at the slippery edges,
empty as bottles found at sea without the hoped-for messages,
all those women are gone inside the women who no longer see you or
        wait for you,
images that the penumbra of the movie theater leads into a hazy
        and bitter focus,
in the place where sorrow spoils any astonishment.

The ring where you fought for so long is now old,
old like your tired heroics;
how many cream pies are made out of it, yet no one has the grace
you had for smashing them into their faces.

But now let's consider the empty ring,
as we step out of the floodlights; let's observe
the empty white surface. Let's watch,
simply, the dice rolled onto that surface or card table,
simply, the dice rolled,
and the players that may be left, unseen
because they sit in the dark, looking at their dice.
In such motionlessness, which besides is the only explanation for
        movement, the only pattern where movement is cast,
we will sense your slow disappearing,
no longer able to float or steer;

disappearing off to all the edges and points of that table or surface
    about to light up,
yet at an infinite distance from that table
where movement starts up again, though the pattern remains.
An infinite distance from the rattling dice that repeat the play,
associating again the deep valleys of your sleep
with some mountain where the dice nurse
the emptiness around that gradually appears.

Trapped inside the hole you have become,
unable to get out, you make it past the rattle of the dice
    that go on rolling on the table long after you have got up,
when all you do is drift toward a spot where emptiness is visible;
an infinite distance from the woman who sings an old foxtrot,
    Night and Day, for example,
next to the piano in some bar
—if such a scene can ever be repeated—
an infinite distance from the song and the elaborate voice
    "the stuff
that dreams are made of..."

translated by Ernesto Trejo

28

(drawing by José Luis Cuevas)

someone moves,
someone is weaving the bottleneck cold,
the floating bottle that evaporates
communication's letters,
the stroke that bends
under the image's weight
where the line
absorbs
all he desired to say of space,

someone observes
the mirror weaving,
perhaps his face
above his face in a blind
arriving later

someone who after checking the pantry
offers his statues a place at the table,

someone is moving,
someone brings the key to the reflection's hole
and the Embottled appears
with his chair approaching the crowd...

(and thus the Indian ink productions
portray less visible transit,
beasts of another reunion stalking a vacuum
through the keyhole)

translated by Sandro Cohen

(the drowned)

                    an iron hook
                    is pulled
          contradicting his size as he emerges
                the water dripping
                     moves
                      him
                     from
                      the
                    threads
            of his entrance onto the stage

                  on the dock the crowd
                  was watching that bundle
              where everyone's eyes awaited
              the body's lost passage

                drop by drop the body fell
                into God's pool,
          someone asked for an iron hook
                to hoist him,
          careful—said one of the onlookers—
          the tide is dragging him under
          the dock,

                    an iron hook
          we had to fasten him with a hook
          we had to tell him something with a hook
          while the dirty floating bundle
                      fell
                     drop
                      by
                     drop
          from where the missing
          would fling a stone upon us,

                              translated by Linda Scheer

(Vía Veneto)

I want to be alone,
the table is cleared,
things need encysted labyrinth space
in the resistence of
I want to be
      alone,

the place where they keep
the tables and chairs
after the meeting,
     an orchestral composition
with the secret glands of
I want to be
      alone,

capricious fly sketches
    creating silence,
they open fire amid the noise of tables and chairs,
everyone speaks at the same time
repeating the discourse of
I want to be
      alone,

      orchestral composition
power-lobes to fertilize
these objects of I want to be alone,

charity spills her dragonflies
    in granite slabs,
the acts of her last will,
    I want to be alone retreats
into the infected latrine effluvium.

translated by Sandro Cohen

JOSE EMILIO PACHECO (1939—), Mexico City.

Pacheco is a many-faceted author: novelist, essayist, critic, journalist and short story writer. He is a natural poet and the synecdochal poet of this anthology as he deals primarily with temporal transition, and capturing the moment is his stock in trade.

Pacheco's poetry espouses a basic concept of existence: time. This abstraction, which stamps all of his writing, is diluted with the concrete and circumstantial passage of the space/world in which he (un)lives, delights and suffers. He achieves dialectic synthesis by embodying his poems with intimate moments which—in the literary circles of the last fifteen years— signify tradition and innovation, permanence and change, certainty and risk.

In Pacheco's "time," one can note the flux and the inevitable reflux of elements which the poet assumes as a naturally tragic error and, at the same time, as the historic "horror" due to constant irrational (nocturnal) transformation; existence seen as the tide that rises, condemned to break and recommence interminably. This Heraclitean conscience alone, however, neither saves nor condemns humanity: destruction and creation without respite are a fatal design which the poet humanizes as he dramatizes it: what, in principle, is guilty simply because it exists, later becomes the inter- changeable victim and the executioner; change is the sentence one suffers, and Pacheco's writing becomes more concrete because of it, more tangible in accordance with the reality of the moment. This is tantamount to the commitment to seize history while taking part in it; his poems carry the weight of a collective consciousness, at times like Sisyphus' rock, and at others like a Rosetta stone that seeks to decipher reality with an igneous accusatory finger.

Pacheco's language has an extraordinary congruency with his tem- poral moments. From a rhetorical language, filled with transparent meta- phors, he leaps to a flexible and simple language which is transformative to the point of being experimental; from elemental and lasting images, he passes to a direct, explicit and fleeting communication; from a classical tone reminiscent of Los Contemporáneos he arrives at an ironic, critical, and even antipoetic tone.

Pacheco enjoys a cultural assimilation which has permitted him to digest the diverse influences of English, Italian and other world literatures and has enabled him to recreate the works of poets who have been funda- mental to his formation.

In his poetry, as well as in his prose, Pacheco's basic obsession is in constant struggle with an ethical/esthetic synthesis: a writing of conscience

33

where lyricism only figures as a lucid recurrence to what was once a more natural and clean world, since the one he observes and survives is inevitably destined to "the ruin of the species." Perhaps this is why he most recently has dealt with the child's world and with the animal kingdom. These are truly masterful poems relating an allegorical zoo of human dimension which we are happy to be able to include in this selection.

Published work: Los elementos de la noche (1963); El reposo del fuego (1966); No me preguntes cómo pasa el tiempo (1969); Irás ya no volverás (1973); Islas a la deriva (1976); Al márgen (1976); Jardín de niños (1978); Ayer as nunca jamás (1978).

THE CLIMBING VINE

Green or blue, the wall's fruit, it grows;
a line between earth and sky.
With time
It becomes stiffer, a deeper green,
habit of stone, a lustful body
with arms intertwining and touching,
they share the sap
each a small plant
but yet a forest;
they are the years,
entangled and broken,
they are the days
the color of fire
they are the wind
that fills the autumn
and touches the world,
the dark roots of death
descendants of a darkness
that rose from the climbing vine.

translated by Ernesto Trejo

GIFT OF HERACLITUS

But water spreads down the windows
like moss:
it doesn't know that everything
is altered once it leaves the dream.

And the fire's repose means assuming a form
out of its full powers of transformation.
Fire of the air, the fire's solitude,
igniting the air made of fire.
Fire is the world that goes out and burns
again to last (it was always so) forever.

What is scattered today comes together,
what is near goes away:
it was and it wasn't me who waited for you
one morning at the deserted park;
I stood by the everchanging river
as it was entered (it will never happen again)
by October's sunlight, filtered
in shattered pieces through the thicket.
There was a smell of ocean: a dove
caught fire in the air like an arch of salt.
You weren't there, you won't be,
but the waves from a distant foam
came together in my deeds and words
(never belonging to others, never mine):
the sea which is pure water to the fish
will never quench the thirst of men.

translated by Ernesto Trejo

4

When light unfolds
it assumes the shape
of what the eye
is inventing.

translated by Ernesto Trejo

DON'T ASK ME HOW TIMES GOES BY

En el polvo del mundo se pierden ya mis huellas;
me alejo sin cesar.
No me preguntes cómo pasa el tiempo.
LI KIU LING *(tr. Marcela de Juan)*

Winter descends on the house where we lived
Flocks of birds angle south
Springtime will come again
The flowers you planted will revive
But you and I
will never see again
the sweet place that was ours.

translated by Ernesto Trejo

FOOTNOTE TO JORGE MANRIQUE

The sea
  is not death unfolding
    but the eternal
      flow of
        transformation

translated by Ernesto Trejo

A LECTURE ON CRABS

On the coast they say that the crab
is a bewitched animal
unable to turn his head
to see where he has been.

The stubborn seas taught him
the art of retreating
he hides
among rocks and mud.

He walks on a slant
and in the tenacity of his pincers
he holds the vacuum, penetrated
by those eyes, ferocious as horns.

A nomad in the mud or a resident
in two exiles:
a foreigner
to water creatures
and to land animals.

A night climber,
wandering armor,
gloomy and forever on the run
he goes on, avoiding immortality
in impossible square circles.

His fragile shell
gives easily to breaking
and incites
our stamping on him.

(In that way Hercules avenged the bite,
and Juno, who had sent the crab against this obscene
circus character,
this charlatan of the heroic age,
got even by placing Cancer
among the twelve signs of the Zodiac,
so that his legs and pincers

40

would guide the sun through the summer
—the time when seeds germinate.)

I don't know when he gave his name
to the tumor that breaks the tissues
which even at the beginning of the last third
of the twentieth century
remains undefeated
and just the mention of which
is enough to send fear
across the face
of everyone present.

translated by Ernesto Trejo

MIRROR OF ENIGMAS: MONKEYS

The monkey is an organized
sarcasm upon the human race
HENRY WARD BEECHER

When a monkey stares at us
we shiver
and wonder
if we're not
in his hall of mirrors
his buffoons

translated by Ernesto Trejo

SCORPIONS

The scorpion woos his mate.
They lock pincers and stare at each other
through a whole sullen day or night.
before the odd copulation
when the marriage is consummated.
The male succumbs
and is devoured by the female
who (said the Preacher)
is more bitter than death.

translated by Ernesto Trejo

THREE CANADIAN POEMS
I
THE STRAIT OF GEORGIA

The woods face the sea
    Above, an eagle
on the tip of the pine
    It was dusk.
The sun sank
    on Vancouver Island

Perhaps it was the Aztlán of the Mexicas
    From there, seven tribes departed
and one
    founded the Aztec empire

Only certain names remained of Aztlán
    sown in the coast
like rocks

The eagle was found in the weeds
    not heraldic
not burning in the dusk
    In decomposition

Fed on fish
    which pesticides, garbage
industrial wastes poisoned

Over Vancouver eagles no longer fly
    Today people
see monsters on the beach

The Aztecs believed that the Sun God
    night after night
died in the form of an eagle
    traveling through the Land of the Dead
to reappear the following day
    (fortified by human blood)
as a jaguar in the middle of the skies

The Indians of Vancouver live
       in The Musqueam Reserve
where the Fraser surrenders the sweet waters
       of the mountain to the sea
which opens its wings

The Strait of Georgia unites and separates
       Aztlán from the continent
the Aztec paradise dead as Tenochtitlán
       city of the moon's navel

In The Musqueam Reserve
       there are three golf courses
The ancient lords of the earth
       carry sporting goods
of the sea monsters

The eagle descends
       has the jaguar drunk the blood of the night?

translated by Michael Rieman

PHYSIOLOGY OF THE SLUG

The slug
    a tenuous creature
takes delight
    in dauntless gardens
He has the moisture
    of moss
the wateriness
    of a life
that never quite began
    He is only
a delicate
    snail-in-project
a premonition
    of something
about to exist
    In his sluggish paradise
of drivel
    he proclaims
that to go about in this world
    means
shedding hunks of ourselves
    here and there
along the way
The slug wears out
    while circling
his own spiral
    On his back he carries
his paranoia
    his overwhelming
existence
Nobody likes
    this insipid pest
that pities himself
    as he crawls on the ground
or climbs walls
Poor thing
    so superstitious
he fears
    (rightly so)

that somebody
    will come
and pour salt on him

translated by Ernesto Trejo

AUTUMN AFTERNOON IN AN OLD COUNTRY HOUSE

In the adjoining room someone is coughing
I hear a muffled cry
Then, someone paces back and forth
a whispered conversation

Very quietly I get closer
and open the door

Just as I feared
        just as I knew
                no one's here

What went through their minds when they heard me?
Are these ghosts afraid of me?

translated by Ernesto Trejo

OLD FOREST HILL ROAD (TORONTO)

Street in shadow
    and winter lowers
        its frozen light in squadrons
Leaves still green in the field
                signs
that autumn
        did not adjust its cycle
Houses closed and in silence
                  enigmas
of so many lives already passed
                  (and others
which will pass)
        but not for me to see
how they passed
        For I was not
nor will be there
        I have come
only in passing
        to this city
to this world
        I am a foreigner
in this land
        In all lands
I will be a foreigner
        When I return
my country
        will have changed
And I will not be
        nor was I there
My only land
        is an alien street
of leaves still green
        which autumn surrenders
to deep winter
        and its frozen light

translated by Michael Rieman

49

EYES OF THE FISH

At the shoreline
the sand-curve
and a row of dead fish

Like shields after battle

With no trace of suffocation
or apparent decay

Sea-polished jewels
Sarcophagi
enclosing their death

There was something
ghostly
about those fish

They had no eyes

A double hollow in their heads

As if their bodies
could be of the earth

But their eyes are the sea's

And the sea observes through them

When a fish dies in the sand
Its eyes evaporate

But at ebb-tide

the sea recovers
what it calls its own.

translated by Michael Rieman

GALDOS

In his last years
there was grief
hardening of the arteries
and a painful blindness

If that weren't enough
the hatred
of half of Spain
and the indifference
of the other half

They snatched away
the Nobel Prize
and mocked
the "smell of chickpeas"
found in his books

He suspended this torture
by taking rides around Madrid
alone

From the coach
he sensed the atmosphere
and in his solitude
his characters, who made
this world more real
came to inhabit him

It was a sluggish
process
by which at last
he became
one more of his creations

translated by Ernesto Trejo

JARDIN DE NINOS: 17

. Like hunks, off the broken statues unearthed in holy cities,
so are the sad toys, the photos, the worn notebooks
that turn up one day in the house.
These ruins are all that remain of the childhood that never comes back
(The statue can be put together again; anyone who looks
behind him becomes a pillar of salt)
Among the debris—or memories—, for one second
the past splits open and then is sealed forever.

translated by Ernesto Trejo

GRAFFITI

In every pencil wood and lead come together; they join
to sacrifice themselves as they create words, numbers,
lines.

A pencil wears away like the hand that leads it.

It dies as it gives birth to markings though it lives on
in them—but these don't last either.

Like wind over sand or rain upon water.

Nature, defeated, speaks through the heavy tongues of
pencils.

A pencil is a tree recently cut down; when you sharpen it,
the shavings smell like a forest.

A pencil, to become a pencil, and out of the habit of
being a pencil, must no longer be wood and lead.

Potentially, it can express anything the mind and the hand
are capable of.

But, unsure, it carries its antithesis at the other end:
the eraser.

All that we and our pencils write is temporary.

Everything must wear away in order to be.

translated by Ernesto Trejo

FRANCISCO HERNANDEZ (1946–), San Andrés Tuxtla, Veracruz.

*A passionate cineaste, Hernandez presently works as a copy-writer. His book,*Mar de fondo, *won the National Prize for Poetry in 1982.*

Inherently doubtful, he resolves his propensity for what is tragic with a special humor, quite unusual in authors of his "generation." Black humor dressed with irony is a constant element in his first texts, which take us back to the mythology of the film noir of the 40s, without reaching the extreme of the black bile of cruelty and sarcasm. Subtlety is his dose of irony, and this irony is what constitutes a true critique of themes that could tend towards solemnity: the love relationship, life/death, and literature itself. Because he is gifted with a facility for "bad blood," his texts cohere by means of a language that is direct and of great impact, filled with cutting and polarized images.

At a second glance, his newest texts acknowledge the influence of a "Lezamalimian" lyricism in metaphoric prose poems that give us a play of secondary meanings that field their principal motivations.

Books published: Gritar es cosa de mudos (1974); Portarretratos (1976); Cuerpo disperso (1978), Mar de fondo (1982)

THE OLD MAN AND THE GUNPOWDER

Old Ernest
placed his forehead
against the barrels
of his shotgun
closed his eyes
saw a lion approach
and fired

translated by Linda Scheer

THE DREAM AND THE VISION

Edgar Bruno awoke
and said: I am
a child and I know
I will never write like Borges
but he is blind
and I know they never
allowed him to be a child

translated by Rochelle Cohen

POST CARD FROM MADRID

death came
and carried away picasso's eyes
decorated by himself
it was sunday
faces were sad
and became questioning
in all of spain
a deep preoccupation emerged
concerning the soccer scores

translated by Linda Scheer

THE POET WHO PLAYED THE FLUTE

under the sharp sun of the archaeological zone
he found it anchored to the soil its form that of a
tigress in the shape of a flute with mouth and pores
open later helped by shaking fingers he erased its
ages of dust and the memories of thousands of loving
lips in the privy house which is the pyramid they became
balls with death they sacrificed cathedrals they filled
the maidens with gold they stirred up the silence of
the helmets with the zero air of tomb seven he raised
the non-existent bauble and blew between its thighs
for the first time: large adorned flys came out
awkward old decisive clear round frozen and blueish
music came forth beautiful like she alone neither
rats nor girls nor gods followed him but the timely
encounter with what is beautiful (or the delayed
effect of the marihuana) made him slip in the middle
of the great stairwayyyyyyyyyyyyyyyyyyyyyyyyyyyyyyy

translated by Linda Scheer

60

FROM THE EMPTY CAGE

a song soared
from the empty cage

the poem is a canary
plumed with words

how to say that the song escapes from the cage
only to be trapped in silence?

***

when he sings
the bird in the cage
becomes visible

the eye is the cage of a voice
liberated in a glance

silence
is a canary imprisoned
within a word

***

from one cage to another
tongue's canary
escapes

new york sings
in its garbage cage

new york's song is the fire
the hoses' streams
are the bars that enclose it

central park
green canary
that believes it is singing
in the arteries
of a smoke stone

the canary doesn't sing
the song sings

the song doesn't end
the canary shuts its memory

***

empty cage
caged song

silence sings in the empty cage

its shadow
the canary's
mute song

in the big cage
lightning's plumed song
thunders

within the song
silence flies in circles
like a caged tiger
feeding on canaries

translated by Linda Scheer

MUSIC BY MAHLER

The first day of the world awakens
the skeleton's razors are sharpened
the submerged part of the iceberg bleeds
and so there is no sea that is worthy
nor fauna that flowers
nor definite color
for naked skin
silence
a white and hard wind
crashes the crosses
of the cemetery
the canals' water
hits the sleeping heart
insistently
silence
loud reds
inside of seashells
lanterns
in the ghost's hand
victory's mane
in light's mouth
silence
nothing like your chiaroscuro
for death
or innocence
silence
as if it were
the last day of the world
music's mind
in my hands
becomes dust

translated by Linda Scheer

SUNDAY

I like the pets
Of the beasts' house of your soul.
Tristan Tzara

Besides rats, there are children in the park. Like them I would
like to be under the sky and run from one thigh to another without
previous itinerary. But I am like the rats, in the shadows, and when
I bite a slice of jicama I bite a small white butterfly. The mineral
blood of the forest flows through my skin. Birds see me and fly a
yawn. In the pond's rotten water, clouds are the remains of some
recently sunken fire. The heat is blue, like Sunday. And a large
drop of sweat crosses my belly reminding me of a dead girl's kiss.
In the distance, the nauseating walls of Mixcoac are beaten by the
sea. I'm so alone that anyone would say you're with me. An
airplane passes so close that it takes away your last words. But
even so, the city is a miserable fire-swallower preventing the
flight of the yellow corollas.
In which swamps are you disseminating your orgasms?
I laugh at those walking their lovers and their dogs because I have
neither dog nor lover to bark at me. I sweat thousands of drops.
Shall I walk at dusk on the water? I sniff among the sewers and meet
a child who has spent her entire life outside. I see your lost glance
and find a dream that is sunstruck under the protection of your memory.
Farther than the horizon someone bandages madness' skull. The
dragonfly escapes from my lips, which means the time has come to
macerate the fly's flesh. Love is what those happy children do not
know. The opposite of love is a reality forgotten in the most loving
part of ourselves.
I clean my nails and tail in the trail left by lovers.
I'm so alone that anyone would say that I shall return to gnaw the
entrails of *the pets of the beasts' house of your soul.*
But no.
I'll never come back.
From my cave I watch as the sun uncovers the earth's crystals and a
dark-haired child tears out a swallow's eyes.

translated by Linda Scheer

UNDER THE VOLCANO

What am I doing here?
What is this frozen fly doing
opposite me
like a girl unknown?
The wind's cadaver
hangs
from the tree's branches.
The toll of the bells passes
in perfect formation.
No one is singing.
No one flies as high as the ants.
Lowry should be here,
under the volcano,
getting drunk from tedium.
The sea, the mezcal, the police,
aren't farther than you.
The ants slowly crawl
up my body.
It smells like a kitchen
and broken silence.
As it crosses my tongue,
light reminds me
of the taste of your
forgotten sex.
We are what the Sleeping Woman* dreams.

*The Sleeping Woman (Ixtaccihuatl) is a volcano in central Mexico.

translated by Linda Scheer

65

ONE

Over remains of drifting light, the sea drops crystals
and the lanceolate precision of its hours. Salty foam
used to abandonment traces kingdom-like circles beyond
the smooth sand.
At the edge of nothingness and the wind, a mirage runs
clear like the shadow of raindrops bursting in the sun.
There are smoking vessels in the wave's restless skin.
Wings that fall fulminated by fish's earthy love.
A seashell approaches the senses and only the sadness
of waves in ruins is perceived.
Day and night disappear. The wind no longer breathes.
The sea calmly contracts, sinks and evaporates.

translated by Linda Scheer

THREE

At the mercy of the north wind and of the voracious
forgetful garden, the Wellingtonia grows.
One is astonished by the intimate trapped light in
its cortex. Its thin voice in the middle of the mist
of a wingless exile is painful. Its transparent
track is renewed on the wall. Its limits from child-
hood endlessly thrive: moss in the statue's cut
finger.
Like a very fine and early limestorm, snow separated
it from the world.
But there are marks of arms that endure in the trunk,
and the other side of delights is discovered in its
blue eyes.
Its sap of words germinates in the cloister's aridity.
Loneliness and death's wink lark in its branches.

translated by Linda Scheer

1

if the hurried kiss
we exchanged
had not tasted
like castor oil to me
I would have raped the pretty
blue-eyed
blue-pantied child

7

on the hands
of those
who have recently died
long
very long
the life line
is seen

9

I throw the word boomerang
and it doesn't return
I take the word valium
and do not sleep
I invoke the word lucifer
and he doesn't appear
I breathe the word oxygen
and am asphyxiated
I caress the word breast
and think of you
I draw the word bridge
and it falls
I write the word final
and begin again

24

the poem
is the only evidence

left by the assassin
at the scene of the crime
(the blank page
is a perfect crime)

translated by Linda Scheer

STREET

This is the street of youth
I am told
and the absence of the elderly moves me
This is the street of firm breasts
and buttocks
and of clean open smiles
of swift strides
of a better angle of hope
so this is the street of the young
I tell myself
and drop my thirty years onto a bench
and try to regain my strength
to continue walking
Havana, October, 1976

translated by Linda Scheer

HOMERO ARIDJIS (1940–), Contepec, Michoacán.

Aridjis served as Mexico's ambassador in Holland and has taught at Columbia University.

A prolific writer, Aridjis embodies the intuitive development of one who, from an early age, decided what his world would be: very much his own, a genuine totality, singular, deserving of his commitment.

His poems, derived from a pristine knowledge—light and shadow, sensuality and dream—contain a certain innocence which is not lost when he confronts reality. This is why they deal with his vision of a world without burdens; his perspective is the blue vision navigating in amniotic liquids filled with light.

Aridjis has a verse which may well constitute the genesis of his work: "there is a body within the body which is the body of all;" life as a continuous flow of love/loneliness, space/absence, time/dream, birds of a blue murmur.

Even when his poetic glance penetrates a circumstantial world, he does not abandon the sensory being par excellence within him; rather, he transforms it into lyrical and amatory playfulness, becoming a tempest of emotion in a pure rain of carnality. Completely disposessed, but for a feeling incapable of hurting, he strips the word to the point of innocuousness.Then, when he speaks of our reality, he is speaking of another entelechy, of one prior, perhaps of one we lost while unaware.

Books published: Los ojos desdoblados (1960); Antes del reino (1963); La difícil ceremonia (1963); Perséfone (1967); Ajedrez/navegaciones (1969); Los espacios azules (1969); Mirándola dormir (1971); El poeta niño (1971); Quemar las naves (1975); Vivir para ver (1977).

BEFORE THE KINGDOM

Before the kingdom
of the floating villages
of the messenger feet
you were already the first shadow
the prophecy unravelling itself
in a slow destruction of angels
you were already the hand   the sword
and the face   both faces
and the belt that binds opposing winds

you were already the last window
the last eyes
the fire of light
the night foul
with the coughing of the sick along the streets

you were yourself
and your double behind like a spy

Before the kingdom
you were not yet you
only premonition
and already you were the presence
the signal like a greeting
the bodies
the copulation falling in pieces

translated by Brian Swann

I'll give you my weapons   the northern wine
distracted stumblings in fear

I'll give you the power of closeness
your image on the roads
and replicas of you in each vision

I'll give you ties   private signs
secret languages so you may speak
in the hostile chamber

I'll give you the domain of the flesh
the face of those who abhor

I'll give you a shared life
for all summer long

I'll give you bodies   distances
herbs for illness
cities overflowing
breeding grounds of silence

Perhaps for a moment you'll start the perpetual smoke

translated by Maxine Adler-Pou

Night dies over a broken apple

Creation begins again

Dawn grows enormous
in her compacted agitations

Man explores memory
and opens the new moment
with transparent hands

Everywhere the fantasy
of being between the hours
the feat the cry the resurrection

Also from the damp earth
from the now hidden events
movement arrives
the perpetual second
the presence

One word cuts your lips in two

translated by Maxine Adler-Pou

before he dies the old man sees a young man approach
his bed
and before the old man dies the young one places his mouth
over his mouth and takes in the moans the words the
sighs
he takes him in once and again for a long time till the old man
expires and the boy is more alive than ever
as he has fulfilled the rite called supplanting the breath of life

translated by Maxine Adler-Pou

he had a vial where he kept algae
and minute dolphins that awoke with the light
and he had a glass tube through which he blew and filled
the air with blue specs and white bugs
and he had a cane he would twirl with one finger and
it grew longer and longer   till when it was pointed toward
night you could see through it a glorious face in the center
of a star   and on the face just one eye that would
put us to sleep at the first look

translated by Maxine Adler-Pou

Faster than thought the image moves
rising in a spiral round   within your body
like sap or tunic or ivy of sounds

Faster than day your glance
cornering hours and abandoning echoes
nests and words of creation stirring

Faster than the image the image moves
that seeks you in light's chasms that is shadow
and finds you visible in the invisible
like someone that living shines

Behind time and before the image moves
Inside the image another image moves
Faster than speed thought moves

translated by Brian Swann

In the hand air

in the eyes sun
that leans on the fire
to last beyond its own rays

around a being
that carries its prison in life

above
the angel of descending water
smashing birds against rocks

in my image
this body of desire
watching the wall

dripping like a roof

the hour rains

a rainbow is born
between sky and earth

translated by Brian Swann

Angels feel themselves in light

they shine invisible between
the seeing and the seen

they leave in the sky
a very clear trace

and in the trees
an open fruit

in eyes that beget
a dream-like being

and in the heart a joy
resembling themselves

the fruit dawns in the tree
full of life-silences

from its moistness arises
some likeness to this dream

beneath the sun
alone and hanging and luminous it waits

it is invisible juice in its juice

translated by Brian Swann

the song under the mist
lights a road
in its drift

dawn opens in a bird's nest
light

the sun
watches the poem
already alive

the fruit
watched
becomes heavy

it moves its shadow
in the tree

translated by Brian Swann

Woman goes naked under each glance
and man divines her

as one flesh they sit beneath the light
in their live bliss

their communion is consecrated
and they offer their blood to drink from it

love is in their faces
and man on earth is accursed

translated by Maxine Adler-Pou

Like the earth
tormented by the rays
but blue over the clouds
she
behind her tormented brow
looks at deathless space

translated by Maxine Adler-Pou

DAVID HUERTA (1949–), Mexico City.

Huerta currently writes literary essays for several magazines and cultural supplements and was awarded a Guggenheim Fellowship in 1978.

The express purpose of this young poet's writing would seem to be to explain the NCF (new conceptual focus) theorized by Barthes. His use of language is directed towards a discursive totality which seeks to break with traditional molds. In this respect, his most recent writing demonstrates an experimental nature and a radical critical essence towards language; his work is open to meanings in an essentially tragic "style:" writing condemned to name and then immediately destroy what is named. It is a language of innovation that takes on "a form that does not contain a meaning but rather a form in search of meaning,"[1] and which "threatens with a secret."[2] Nonetheless, the anxiety of a rhetorical shipwreck is felt, placing his poetry in a constant risk, adrift, in a struggle to break away from an inherited language, to renounce accumulations which do not authenticate him. That is why, in his poems, Huerta does not speak of something but rather for something: to destroy one world of words, to create another that will once again "explain" reality to us by means of his way of seeing it.

Huerta's poetic trajectory clarifies his essential search and certainty to us. In his first book, El jardin de la luz, he ontologically asks himself about what he will later answer: "is it morning or dusk?" This awakening inscribes his look in a formal tradition while his poems aspire to a metaphoric conciseness and to an autonomy of exactness.

His writing spills over densely like an oil lamp that illuminates the space in which he writes: shadows in which he intermittently affirms and then denies himself. The meaning of his writing becomes apprehensible to the reader only due to the capacity of the reader's eye to retain it within the vertigo of his writing.

Huerta seems to illuminate a space of no one, a neutral space, with the beam of light of one who throws it afar, to the future. Among the young poets, he is the one who best aims towards a new poetic tautology: perhaps it is the destiny of his marginal look; to discover the dark course of what is to occur, as Lezama Lima wished to do (and did).

Books published: El jardin de la luz (1972); Huellas del civilizado 1977); Cuaderno de noviembre (1976); Versión (1979)

1. Octavio Paz: Poesía en movimiento.
2. Roland Barthes: Writing Degree Zero.

RESIDENCE

Thin shadow,
mirrors sloping.
A flower of tranquility
matures in intimate foliage.
From the air's fountain
comes this silk light.
Breeze's kingdoms
commence their tenuous
labyrinth. Is it morning
or dusk? Instant's
weightless itinerary;
devotion bearing
flights of birds. Dust
is an opaque reverberation
under this sky
of felt presence.
The look shines
in the center
of silence.

translated by Linda Scheer

GARDEN

*"Afternoon, incomplete sphere constellated
by light..."*
                    Joes Emilio Pacheco

Rectilinear moisture
generously given by the afternoon
is a memorable sensation
under the amber sky.
The tacit perfume
which the garden unfolds
submerges memory
in a turn
of transparency.
Like a surge of waves
sealed and detained
by afternoon's light,
the world, hypnotized,
yields to this power
that imposes slowness
on time's things.
The garden, clearly,
is already in the past:
hemisphere of existence
exhuberant and minimum;
herbarium of magic
before the depth
of the suspended look.

translated by Linda Scheer

III

Image
upon image:
fire
has taken
the form
of your shadow
under the moon.

translated by Linda Scheer

DETAILS

for Victor and Juan

at water's edge
        drowsiness
circa 1972:
        ...ho, & a bottle of rum/
at sleep's edge
        golden water
broken doors
I walked in circles
the park was destroyed
under the rain of nickel
broken windows

a name written on the glass
with trembling fingers
my sadness shone in night's hands
harsh hands of intoxication
...and a New Year's celebration
/ho, & a bottle of rum/
quotations from Villiers
a poem by cummings
"somewhere I have never travelled
gladly beyond any experience
your eyes have their silence"

what a disaster the family said
and it was true
beyond any experience
happily
burnt glass
        splinters in my eyes
in the midst of a faint
and above revolved a lyrical moon
caressing my hair with fingers of mercury
what a disaster I agreed

and then Blake's drawings in the Frick Collection
primordial guilts innocence and sleep's splendor
but that slice of life was also true

90

behind my irritated pupils a memory
an almost erased intimate sign
due to monstrous pills

so much reading in the garden in the living room
the caress of a silent hand
we studied till dawn
laughin' & grip
the no-doze pills wet with reflections
the talk in the swimming pool of sleepless fire

and I ready for any vagary
happily beyond any experience
sunken in the Great Ignorance
open-mouthed in the midst of everything

aha, they said, look this way
                    smile
                        sing

the photos don't yellow
but the city crumbles with sweet violence
it's neither the end of the world nor the beginning
they say it's worse to go on like this
and then the streets the posters the cries
and Under The Asphalt Is The Beach, the riots and
the splendor of the police cars announced
everyone's horrible humiliation
but we were hoping for something else
a diluted hope after so many blows
until afternoon almost evening in the plaza
a demonstration of strength
and, they said, the core of subversion has been
        suffocated

the newspapers we anxiously bought
a stain-like fear in each corner
in each gesture

and friends went from one topic to another
I didn't know what to say
except what time is it? who said that?

Oaxaca during the Eclipse
the rainbow hues of the Market
youth's invasion of the streets
a piece of cheese and a bottle of wine
"guilty cigarettes rolled
and furtively smoked at the highway's edge"
Miahuatlán and telescopes
                    fragments of movies
and then the ascent to the city-temple
I thought I'd write a poem about Montealbán
(and I wrote it, oh!: it's dedicated to Paulina Lavista)
the delirious return on the sleeping highway
hallucinated by two days of partying
abused by the effort

circa 1972 (and even before, during 1971) I saw myself
                    in the mirror
with a deep mistrust
            with Enormous Fear
puddles obliquely arranged by the drunkedness
how funny I said, and how sad,
and the parties where I knew no one
the overwhelming parties
the hellish three-day parties
dumfounded
            undeceived
                    hypocritically alone
with nocturnal fears at suicide's edge
and a not too tragic fury when I arrived home
lies
        secrets
            deformations

everything together in front of me
before my useless hands and my ineptitude to "continue ahead"
as everyone recommended
but where was *ahead?!*

at rain's edge
I happily would eat anything
beyond any experience

as if nothing had happened
without wanting to come out of all this
I cried with a harsh gesture of despair
not too tragic

I was here or there I don't know
I lost my eyeglasses I broke them
                              what do I know (shit)

at the edge of a darkened glass
spitting teeth
my breast saturated by lunar signs
completely drunk
and writing poems about Light Afternoon
Water Time as if all of this
were material for celebration or contemplation
I also lost my money
and was mugged one dawn

at water's edge
by this vicious light by the moment
whose name is Suffering

isolated for 25 minutes
completely out-of-it
to be-to have-to have / a poem by cummings
a paragraph by André Breton
counting coins in the shadow of the city-sleep
and the mercurial light *so* lovely and *so* deep

I remember now López Velarde's poem
("the deadest of dead seas")
enraged by used things by things
that are insidiously inert
and peaceful and with quotations on hand
during that argument about poetic
meanings (oh)...//

rest is there in a jug of water
in a garden on the beach in music obsessively heard

at the edge I say this & that
at the worn edge I walk

I stumble into a statue of ash
I look at everything with difficult gestures

translated by Linda Scheer

There is a small prophecy in the air's poorest wall,
the young awaken in another dream, slide their unreal hands
        under habit's utensils,
say enormous yellow words, bite the food sprouting from autumn's
most nutritious and terse instant, in the light "of that time."
Brief and splendid things, phrases that extend secretly
in the midst of parties cooked in the penumbra of immobility
containers quietly sealed,
minute sprouts, apparitions in a disconcerting surface:
these "noble realities" move the gentleman scattered
on the quay of immobility, in the liquors of what is fixed,
fascinating flights, motionless ruins, stone-like moments that suffice
        to establish the terrible vacation
of a phantom taking the sun in our mouth, by chance.

Common day is twisted here, it's a delicious thing to see,
a peaceful monster, a languid notebook.
The passage from there to now is audible, mirror incrustations
        return it
to its hollow tunic, its wounded oils. But the day knows more than
        we, it's a different foliage
it has noble gardens, springs hidden in its arms of felt;
instruments, pills for the surgery of the unnamed,
display windows of exhaltation for the subtle breast of the restless,
corners of arid bodies, collections of evidently atrocious hair,
sad objects that would tear us down.
The day observes the passage, the citizen dissolves in the suit of his
        meditative smoke,
and the small artesanry of immobility surrounds all our questions.
What should happen in rest's cascade? We shall look at the enclosed
        circle, the girded figure: it's not enough,
it's necessary for the splinter to endure, if not the house would enter
        the ceramic of immobility,
in its turbid tinctures, in its deaf summer.

What is the nyctalops like? It has cubes, edges, hair, blood
        of eyes in its eyes, and in its look
that crosses the jungle of immobility like a wasp it would perforate
        the flagstones of the moral nose.

The nyctalops knows, suffers or moans, always the same, in its
    ceiling of fire, in its seal of tepid guitar,
with its arms open to its foam-like blood, with its eyes melted in
    what it sees, and as it sees it stammers.
(But there are things that interest the women of oceanic backs
    and this is spoken of only reticularly;
this is spoken of only in the thick collision of dawn
and in the congregations of a soft voice;
because now the white shadow of what is comfortable-clear
is not what interests us, rather the toy of endurement,
the laugh of a stone, the inclemencies and black sparks of the
word *no*).

This is what is harsh, the tight ring: the rigour of asphyxiation and
    burning dragged along by perfection,
the harmonic course and the turbid tinkling of the arpeggio:
but these matters have a separate garden, they graze on burnt glass,
ingest their images filled with generosity and "respectful
    distance,"
return their transformed and fertile images with the dangerous
    gesture and aplomb
of a discursive tyranossaurus: Not this, these images
have their own provision, their celestial mouth
their shared stomach; these images
cultivate their perfect pasture in slopes of unconquerable and *blinding*
    light.

Meagre film of immobility, barely in the sleep
of a word that has an entry in the dictionary, and it is the word
    same.
But there is something in another word, an enemy of the latter which we
    won't repeat and which is filled
in its celebration of mercury there, against that word of an infinite
    lexicon and brightness of mirrors strung together,
we will write that other word, the one which is heard and provokes
the worry and sickly anguish that we are all familiar with in
    the extended kingdom of immobility:
this is the equivocal and unanimous word: the particle *oneself*.
We have touched this word's marrow so many times; let no one say this
    is not so, so that this word should not echo faithfully.

96

Someone awakens from his sleep, approaches the pieces of his sleep,
but finds this word intact and disproportionate: he awakens, awaken.

Afterwards, someone feels that around the corner is the beast of
        immobility.
But his story is difficult to tell and pronounce like certain words;
resonant, attractive, frightful and illustrious words: obstacle,
        rainbow-hued, metallurgy.
This story, nonetheless, hides in a fiber of the small prophecy
which is now, without anyone's knowledge, without even the glass and sandal
        of perception brushing it,
on a wall, which is air's poorest wall: it remained there.

In the city of our hands a person drowns, splashes frantically,
        picks up dust, curls up and cries. Who is he?
In the vocabularies of the letter he hides, flees, and becomes sick,
endlessly convalesces, but continues fleeing,
another person; and the masks turn green. Something is hiding from us.
But what is it? In the lines of a lamp, in the cortex of a spark,
in the gold mines of a micron, a person discovers all his blood
outside, there: in the drought of immobility.
How has it happened? So many questions and how to come out of them,
        of these streets as well,
of the very Same excessive and deaf, unending city;
of the forgotten diminutions governed by the penumbra, each corner of
        ourselves put in bet's fire,
in the laugh or "in desolation;"
or perhaps ask the nyctalope, who shuts himself up now
in an overflowing rainy telephone booth, talking to whom,
        telling him everything.

translated by Linda Scheer

Today is a threshold and immediate possibility, haste and writing,
fear of lacking due to "inexactness" or a wait, irremediably found
      in others,
appetizing sound of cats on lets, machines fading away,
absolutely personal blood, rage and a smell of use
and wardrobes that stood out vainly in the fresh space...
That is what weighs with sweetness and an imprecise marker in the calm
      breast,
while with profuse slowness the body's rectilinear respiration
      is heard:
a burning vestige in the drought, in the necessary table of feeling or
      dreaming,
far from the posters of lasting autumn you progress farther or nearer
      to your "desire;"
something that made the inextinguishable stairway wound in the
      corridor of the dreaming person...
But at times direct conspiracies, vile merchandise emerge from the
      dream;
sleep transforms lung's night into a pasture of sterile orles
and then insidious bitterness and decomposition remain carved there
(and in that long and penetrating minute, shirts give off a
      surprising oil,
glass is there burning with incrustations of blue and round hooks,
rain appears with solemn speed to feign indifference...).
What gives shade and feeling to the threshold's tatoos doesn't deny
      absence;
if you appeared in the wound that would be as if to inhabit it,
your fear was less than the restlesness that pushed you with rage
      and resignation.

translated by Linda Scheer

There is no "language of the look:" it's a stammering.
Nothing is added to the name in the act of watching, nothing to
      the object.
Edge of additions for light deposited in the world by the eye and
returned by the world to the window, where a double navigation
of things is carried out: this, that... *226745*

translated by Linda Scheer

There's something like a strange coating in my mouth, a taste of
    remembrance when I slowly listen to you,
and nocturnal silence rests on my chest in a way that makes me
    withdraw;
then I reject the blue and disconcerting paste of your words
which have extended in a line similar to the color white
through the field of my ears, inside me vertically,
and I think that your voice doesn't belong to me and is only a
    broken, irremediable, distant sound.
(There's a determination of light in the fact that your voice
    doesn't belong to me.)

It would be of no use for me to explore a single peaceful millimeter
    of the night to "calm myself"
or to look for a mask of consolation in the debris I know,
because the city I've searched for in you is a mirror without
    relationship to "sentimental shelters."

Sudden pencils, inks that lose their leaves, pages that emerged and
    notebooks that disappeared:
this I have known; but nothing like your fruits of elongated hearts;
your words that cross the surface of my life and create a space
    where I hear them vaguely,
with a worldly habit, in the midst of so many matters of
    oblivion, and at some time frightened
by memory's voracious substance. Your tenacious use of life
    at my side, waiting and building
the confidence we should deserve like a breath.

translated by Linda Scheer

Afternoon has arrived like an eye of dust, its matter fallen in
    the middle of things,
a climate of transit in the seas of a person and in its white
        foliage,
rectilinear god surviving in day's lake,
interruptions and confinements with their own music;
this is the afternoon, not its sky, not its scenes of peaceful ink,
    of ochers traversed by bitter words,
and not its high hymn of clothing boiling with a stammering of ash.

I've seen the afternoon and its hands of secret earth,
its loyal garbage, the sun that surrounds it and passes like a
        trace of dangerous oblivion
through the siege of houses, through the smoke we would dream,
and I have seen you there, aloof from restlessness,
my eyes in November's water, as if the afternoon were
        an enormous mirror for your life.
These were the images of the afternoon, it held them in its stained gold
        and in its minute and constant root,
and you said long phrases like ferruginous fear,
but what you said was covered with other durations,
time was a continuous residence for the afternoon to pass without
        remonstrances or threats,
and you knew the awakening of another memory, the ways of an element
        which were only for us,
an atmosphere at the bottom of the corridors, an edge of deserted
        burning, a proximity filled with signs.

I've seen the afternoon that was yours, I've heard your breath
        in the contiguous night,
I've tasted the salt of your sadness, I've put my lips where
        you've appeared for me.

I know your habit of coming out behind my obsessions and your
        way of emerging at each question.

But you hide your pain like an unlucky number,
but your dream is farther than my irremediable poverty and
        I know that under the darkness you weep
and speak with another voice which I hear with a face of loss,

a voice that writes an ignored warning on my chest and traces a
    trembling letter
in the cold vessel of my dress. One pain and yet another for the
    city of your strength.

Afternoon is a dark modification, a jetty afire where I've put
    my hands
to stop this day's serum and to approach you, when
    you grow covered
by the cascade of changing signs,
in the metal of light that transforms into a burnt well;
afternoon has a desired boundary,
a beginning of order for us, a new brightness, a different
    fragility.
You should deeply watch the language that is granted,
the designation that sinks in a look.

translated by Linda Scheer

...What hasn't been said is millennial; it's in the heart of a
    silence
aflame as a lamp; the sum of what is relative and of
    what is postponed is writing's tenacity.

translated by Linda Scheer

JAIME REYES (1947–), Mexico City.

Reyes is currently coordinator of cultural activities for the Casa del Lago of the Universidad Nacional Autónoma de México. His book Isla de raíz amarga, insomne raíz, won the Javier Villaurrutia prize for poetry in 1977.

In one corner, where his lonely wolf enters a verbal battle with the social activist, we have, breaking into the literary ring, this gladiator— called a "street fighter" (to differentiate him from the "classical fighters") due to his lack of consideration for his opponent, language. The wrestling tone of this introduction is not haphazard because he risks his mask in each fall, that is to say, in each poem closely linked with the reality it touches: a society of broken relationships in a world obsessed with self-destruction. It does not bother him to dispose of the rules of the game; he knows he is a loser and is determined to sell his defeat dearly in a ferocious surrender and virulent break. His attack on language—symbol of rejected traditions— is the password, and he makes words artifacts of aggression by using another language, subverted from correct speech, while at the same time, a subverter of (his) reality. And so the verbal purveyor of his writing explodes as he opens the dams of expressive censorship deluged with the prosaic torrent of his verses.

Reyes is substantially a poet of the blood, committed to the pain— love, one of the fundamental elements of his texts, and also hate, its opposite and complement—which pierces him in such a drama of cathartic fusion that he makes a critique of the object from the crisis of the subject: love sought after as an act of destruction. Passion sown in a wasteland with a ferocity sustained only by the daily struggle with disaffection, Reyes throws us the foam of the impotency of loving truly. His texts, long and repetitive, resemble the paraphernalian time he names: petrified and voracious, filled with repression and violence, about to be drowned. Nonetheless, his written source of change is rooted in this alluvion.

Book published: Isla de raís amarga, insomne raiz

THE DEFEATED

To Carlos Monsiváis

1

They go backwards, trampling each other,
and only their grimace of pain is important to them.
Like those in love they don't hear, don't see, they're covered with
    dust, old miasma and heat.
They meet under the quays to exchange kisses that taste of tin
    cans and sawdust,
and take each other's hands and dance in alcohol's light
and sing and believe in life, but believe in nothing, they're alone,
    alone as only they can be.
They've left the cancer in their parents' necks, and, at times,
in the worm-sleep that fills them they jump up, shout,
    toss about;
but when day breaks they carefully look under the sewers
and then reconcile with everything and think that once again
    they've won.
They're the victims and, since from the beginning they're
    conquered
and know it and laugh at those who think are winning, they're the
    executioners.
They can't defeat anyone, they also know this, and so from the
    beginning they're the victors,
those who always have their way, the sterile,
those who have everything because they've nothing to lose.
Nothing is important to them, they're alone, like madmen, proud,
    shouting,
howling, enraged. Infuriated, they steal busses,
pick up cobblestones, attack and when almost victorious, feel
    impotent.
They know it. They know they can't do anything and so nothing
    is important to them.
Because they've descended to the depths of themselves and have
    found hells,
desolation, the rude laughter of those who proudly love each
    other in the city,
they don't try, they know that everything is useless and that
    nothing will be saved.
They've the certainty of truth seized by the neck, whipping it,

and in it they whip lovers and workers and the good people
        with their shadow of shit behind their children's tracks.
They steal, and know that to steal is to surrender yourself.
They kill, and know that to do so is to give love, love, the
        blessed fire of demolition.
The defeated open their mouths to receive poison,
they open their arms to receive corpses of sand
and they feel happy, intolerably happy.

2

Surrounded by smoke, hearing themselves,
they border the street of sadness, scarcely grazing it.
They shout and are silent over their bodies' bandages,
and love no one nor confide in anyone.
They want to go on alone, but know that they'll continue,
continue falling and rising constantly
over the blood of their parents and brothers and sisters and
        of their assassinated names.
They love each other fruitlessly, not asking or giving anything,
waiting for everyone's last day
and for total silence to cover the windows and curtains and walls.
They see the same scene of a same wait,
and share their discoveries with no one, because in reality they
        discover nothing,
they see within themselves and know that nothing is there
but tombs and fog and a growing darkness
filled with cries and cats and impatience which they drown
in alcohol and drugs that ferment over their bodies.
All outside presence and existence interrupts them, they want
        to see nothing,
they're closed to whatever surrounds them and only want to
        go on being
the green well of insects in which they live.
Trapped by an infernal cry, they sweat and wallow about
and give birth to ghosts and their fever-burnt bodies
        want nothing
but to fight in the peace of their own torture
sought after and pursued and fed by the garbage and scraps
they find around them and wish to be alone.
Insomnia and insecurity and awkwardness reign over the doors
        of their houses,

and a boiling shroud of sand covers them.
Inhabitants of inebriety and of darkness' whirlwind,
they infallibly drag themselves, until one by one, they wound
each place vulnerable to fertility. (And they're completely
      fertile and vulnerable.)
Over the blanket of days they accumulated memories they knew
      to be useless, and
yet, they sometimes cry like children, insatiably,
      when they find themselves dispossessed,
without anything to bring them back to a time or place.
Muttering, in collusion with the science of power, united,
day and night and tomorrow and today they try to go against
      the dog's life that slaps them down.
They're the first to fall under parents' bullets,
and the first to want this to continue, because they know that
      everything is,
finally, useless and absurd.
Conspirators in a false rebelliousness,
one day they awoke feeling impotent and enraged;
and then they proposed to forget and they forgot,
because when they were silent they didn't know what to say
and so they found themselves mute and their hands
      and paws tied,
like deer, to a stone of unforeseen sacrifices.
(They see that no one calls them, but there they go, to give
themselves, knowing they'll be rejected.)
(Mythical, dusty shadows, they threaten to destroy whatever
they touch, touched themselves by the inexorable gift that
destroys and catches up to them.)
      And so they go on to the point of weariness,
until completely exhausted in this endless game.
      Contaminated by the land in ruins in which they were born,
      vainly, hour after hour,
in the smoke, they wanted to clean themselves; but their bodies
      were closed and they found
no answer or exit for this ferocious pain of destruction that
      possessed them.
Barely separated by a thin layer of fear, but far from each
other, in loneliness, like madmen, they uselessly transmitted
      signs that the other wouldn't understand.
But they persisted in the game and couldn't forget themselves,

because as they evoked themselves, knowingly, they destroyed
       themselves.
Unconscious and contradictory, without listening to anything,
       hearing but without understanding
(without understanding each other) they tried to go away and did,
       and when they did they found each other.
Neither they nor those who knew them knew who they were,
that's why they never got anywhere,
because they never wanted to.

3
And when they saw and heard they said nothing;
not even did they move;
but they did roll their eyes about.
Next to them, their children looked at them
and said nothing either
and their looks said nothing,
their looks were transparent
and they were behind their parents
and their parents felt as if someone were banging a nail into their flesh,
but they didn't move or say anything or even cry
or remember the footsteps of the batallions inside their heads
killing people with impunity and openly proclaiming peace.
The only thing they heard was their fingers as they brushed the
buttons, turned on the radio and heard the news.
But they said nothing, asked for nothing that would avoid the killing.
And the young, filthy and long-haired,
hid under the bridges, at the edge of highways,
next to the sleepers of the stations,
and were covered with dust and sewage
and afterwards they became soft, transigent and identical,
and they accepted the establishment,
and their flesh, clothing, their way of talking ant their attitudes were
the fountain of monies for tourism and the president accepted them
and rewarded some of them and they felt happy
crawling again through the streets, in daylight.

translated by Linda Scheer

WITHOUT MEMORY OR OBLIVION

to Rubén Salazar Mallén

1

Rooms upstairs and rooms downstairs,
old bastard, goddamn old man, there's one who disowns you,
one shouting that it's not true, useless stump,
nasty feelingless bastard.
Rooms upstairs, rooms downstairs, goddamn it, I accuse myself of your
  death,
since afterwards, only after me you're no longer possible,
you no longer have a reason to stay up late.
  It's Monday. It's Monday and it's smoky and it's the rotten
  Veracruz land that sucks,
stomped on, ridiculed. Now it's Monday and it's hell.
Lance's point, old disgraced soldier,
cuckholded devil, pot-bellied old man,
what whores will you teach in hell?
who will wipe your drivelling eyes
and your mangy spitting mouth?
I bet you don't know—you, so serene, so objective, inflexible,
rod of killer gasses I bet you don't know what death is like
Downstairs epileptics are dancing,
hemiplegics carrying flowers for you to piss on, good people, bad
  people,
fags and madwomen a chorus you deserve rotting old man, they're
             coming
  to give you glory.
  You're hurting me a lot, so much,
you're hurting me so damn much, imitation of god, human phlegm.
And there are nights when I want to look for you,
blessed john, knocked down fighter.
And there are nights and days when I want to look for you and you
             leave
  me nothing,
devouring heat, book-eating worm you even took my hands with you.
And there are nights and there are days,
such terrible days when I don't even want to get up
because you're dying in my hands,
because you're warming me so with your rotting body,
sweet death, sweet tepid and gangreened death.

111

A tear drops, a drop of blood, of boiling asphalt
to see you, to see your worms' caress on the lukewarm pillow.
A drop of my blood falls, a drop of milk, a drop of quicksilver in the
    wounding streets
to see your lovely eyes, your lovely baggy eyes,
hooded quack.
And I'm getting tired, terribly tired and I'm afraid,
lechery, desperate cries in the empty night
empty, empty like your body, like your food, like your mouthless
    kisses,
without children, the old or prostitutes to guide.
You're hurting me, man, you're hurting me too much, you old bastard.
    They're calling me now. One mustn't make anyone wait.

2
I consecrate you in this hour of infamy.
I refuse you this head of mine that's bursting.
I refuse to believe in your death, I refuse to believe you.
You're now the smell of sex,
caress contracted in the violent pyres.
Wall of the sermon,
naked cockchafer dancing in the darkness
—you indeed on only one foot—
    And there are pieces of glass in buttonholes,
private highways of insomnia on the sidewalks.
I refuse, I refuse with all the force of my rage, of my hatred,
I refuse.
Now you're the key to the constantly conceived instantaneity,
wheels you wheel and which close and are blinded,
since you wanted to act right in spite of yourself and in spite of your
desires.
But there's a stupid coiled-up old man who isn't your father
or your mother on the bookcase staining your large hands with closed
    gallows and purulent debris,
your sweet large hands softened by decomposition.
Fritter of insolation, dream of phantoms,
endless rope, rope of surprises for my heart,
but my heart's a broken mirror,
a deceit uselessly familiar without you.
And you who no longer know what the rain is like from here,
crop of spasm, salt water in the wound, in the eye that's opened

to look at you, to touch your lovely eyes almost asphyxiated,
wall of hope, hope of the wall, not of forgiveness.
If I were once again The Doer, old man,
who once again could make you out of mire and shit, my beloved, my
     dear old man,
my wooden leg in the humid morning.
If I could kill you again for fifteen years,
for fifteen years throw in your face this mud, this dispair,
this thread of drunkenness stumbling in the corners,
pissing on the houses and trees of the world,
old world like your hate or my dispair.

3
I have some sanity left.
Now like then it's useless to expect anything of you.

4
I open my eyes and night bursts in the darkness like the
crack of a whip.
I get up and stumble into my weeping,
with my eyes that lovingly want to keep one of your last worms.
Because you procreated worms, because you gave me neither light nor
     peace.
Because now I carry you as a last lament and I'm happy,
happy to kick your skull and piss on it and drink your milk on it,
dark blood of miseries.
But over your death and my death, my friend,
remains Desire
opaque
but without lines
opaque
but without memory or oblivion.

5
And I am so small that I need to ask you—to know—
what you think of life
and what about death—your death—
now that you're dead and there's no one to kiss you,
not one to visit you in this hour of surrender.

113

6

How you must be laughing now
with your false teeth
and your abandoned fascist shirt
and also your abandoned sickle and hammer
and all, all your abandoned papers
disenchanted child who searched and searched and searched and never
    found anything.
How you must be laughing now at everything I'm saying
because that's how you were,
because only the mangy laugh and the stone laugh
and the truncated laugh and the skeptical laugh were left of your love
before the child who you, before anyone,
old world, old drawers, old despair
knew had no salvation.
How you must be laughing now that I ask you.

7

Here at the same time two men light two cigarettes
and tonight I'll go to bed with Blanca Idalia—sometime friend,
terror's courtplaster, anguish's bandage.
Everything's true, everything's true,
it's true that I love you and that I hate you and that I love myself
like the hook that tears out my palate.
There's no lie possible,
there's no death, we don't throw life away anywhere.
Here at the same time two men light two cigarettes.
Heads or tails: who are you, dead one?
Tonight someone is going to bed with Blanca Idalia.

8

Calm sets in closing your notary's offices,
sealing forever never more your dirty papers that were useless.
Calm sets in.
I want to call your house, to know how the decomposition of your
    body's coming along,
how you stubbornly want to sow a last smell
and a last herd of worms in your bed.
Empty envelopes, also an empty jug and you, unconscious child thrown
    on the bed
dribbling your last words, colossus of ebriety,
eye sockets of the infamies of all, all your world you curse with your
    death.

I want to call your house and the telephone refuses, stops,
challenges me as you would have.

9
You pull yourself from there and they pull you from me,
rotten root, stalk.
I don't want you to die, I don't want it.
If they take you away they're taking away my body,
they're burying me as they bury you.
But as for your death and my death
I'm at a loss.
I clash against the morbosity of your people.
How do they know so much about you? How do they recognize
you now if I myself no longer know you?
I'll shut myself in now and try not to save you
and try not to save you and save you. I'll go to sleep.

10
Someone without your knowledge
without your even realizing it
has put into fashion
paying homage to the dead,
shaking the old corpses in their old mummy boxes on exhibition.
But I don't want to pay homage to you,
or even cry for you because I hate you, I hate you with all my blood
       and hemorrhage,
with all my idiotic laughter and my pretty-girl poses.
If at least, if I could only dig you up with these hands of mine that
       you took with you.
If I could only ask you what children you'll take to fornicate
in hell's brothels.
But nothing. Nothing and nothing and nothing but blood and blood
       striking.
rushing, drowning lives your blood a shroud.
(I said something similar to you when you were alive,
and look how different this can sound to you now,
when you're without me and, lance-point I support myself in you to
       live
because I don't want to shroud you or wash your body
or close your eyes or color your rotted guts again,
water which I didn't dry.

115

I mean you're dead now, quite dead,
but before I knew you you were already rotting and you knew this
there was a reason you sent out old death notices with a loving phallus to
your friends.
There was a reason you asked a batallion of spiders
instead of me to weave you a sweet hammock, forgiveness' last
farewell, chief of calm.
        And so what, so what if before me you were already dead,
if you couldn't even hide your motionless body from me.
So what if you had died before and I had known nothing of you.
Your sickly laugh strikes me
no longer trying to hide evil.
Your books and papers strike me
and the pen you no longer use awakens me each night mockingly, cruel,
tickling my nose to fill me with you now without you, now without
        you
old bastard what balls you had to die,
what balls not to avoid your departure and your awkward adventures.

11
It's late and I have to get some sleep. It's late for everything now.

translated by Linda Scheer

JOSE DE JESUS SAMPEDRO (1950–), Zacatecas, Zacatecas.

A full-time professor of language and literature in the Universidad Autónoma de Zacates, Sampedro won the National Prize for Poetry in 1975 with his book, Un (ejemplo) salto de gato pinto.

His use of language has made him a polemical poet, one who gives polysemic meanings to the literary task.

Armed with a desire to make the poetic idiom equivocal, he seeks to find a rationale for the unconscious; the automatic writing of surrealism is his point of departure, but it is only that: the founding block of his writing that eludes "the accumulation of signs" which an orthodox bretonianism would not avoid. It could be said that his intent is syntactic subversion, as he permits the unconscious —as a poetic category, as an antithesis of formal syntax—to appear. However, he goes further as he proposes to give communicative legibility to what is meaningless.

And so, language becomes an experiment that deals with the scientific "game" in which the subject is inoculated with virus-words and remains silent as he awaits results. The poet enters a vertigo where he does not lose his senses: circumstantial clarity and historic time are present, although confused, not in chaotic darkness but rather in the fusion of different objective/subjective categories which make for a style that is distinctively codified and, at times, telegraphic.

His poetry is not easy, as it is the result of a convulsive experience: language of everyone and of no one and, at the same time, the synthesis of that very language. Poetry that is fleeting and, paradoxically apprehensible. He has made a verbal hell congruent with (his) reality and desire as he proposes a new sensibility where rationale is not enough to comprehend that other reality.

Book published: Un (ejemplo) salto de gato pinto

joe & marilyn

dimaggio couldn't
    connect with that ball
had he made a hit
    well then he would have scored easily
but he didn't calculate sufficiently
    marilyn waits between first
and third neutral
    death is nowhere
suddenly it appears at home
    abandoned

translated by Linda Scheer

the cave of god second printing

juanacatlán death knows you don't
farewell meeting farewell andré breton dear old man
the witch doctor's chimney igneous number follows you
sharp head spec of nose straw ear
finally i assume you magnitude splitting this from
    emptiness
and a probable angora cat
tenderness puts on your broken slippers
don't put your crimson fish into this absurd
    thought
blinking limit distance doesn't succumb
like another the lady mannequin of the supermarket
    courts me
loaf of dead for the bread soup
come with me pretty peach come closer with great
    holiness
let's make love in a dark vestibule
not the smoke flower or the good omen will remain
the mist assures an obscene multicolor evasion
you who ask me for misfortune to put in your
    conspiracy
entrance or exit from the decrepit party
look for your curiosity in the cradle's diapers
the butcher will bring a leg of steam
we'll eat silently watching a red ant
    that climbs you
farewell one day stop-over that fights misfortune
a ticket to the one-eyed of a drawer the unwise asks for
    nothing
you were the conversation of a stiff post in winter
you take your necklace of smiles from the bureau forgive
    the termite
truce not granted or bitter
take off the cover then from the virgin in the patio
    threatened by rain
and stand up death comes untimely
the kiosk of tenderness eats a frightened rabid
    radish
i'll find you in this similar rotten rust

you can come to the lemon juice patio
leave your capricorn house to the hunchbacked violinist
soon the poem will be like the one who rests
        besides this:
myth of chance recent fatality of a closed-off
        stairway
in *juanacatlán* the constant line surprises but no
change of transparencies for a boiling vegetable
baggy eye of the shared secret today burnt
brick fence to stop farewell i love you
madhouse san josé: copper caterpillar:
don't leave me here *cristera* tick i want a
        deaf needle
the storm sleeps at your side the howl rots
        in a cell
of punishment
the dog when it makes love to you and you are awake
in another cell moisture breaks its easter egg
        urine fornicates
the cement bed where cinderella rests
and a chaste priest and a wise cockroach
i affirm that the morning star lives in this
        filthy well
the pestilence of the purple pig seduces me
during christmas i put the moon in my shoe and
        take off the bell
from the perverse saint from the adored saint
come with me pretty one what's invisible is a pomegranate
        i have orange dreams
a scribble is my husband and a burst callus is
        my lover
oh if marta of the stupid sonnambulistic zenith could see
she'd call me jaguar's eye-tooth
now dying quite dying of you timid little animal
a tree slept in the hospital you made coffee
in an empty room your friend drank alcohol
        and laughed
there's no syringe to sleep with you or prick to
        dream of you
like another who was leaving girl who cries for her
        new shadow

i came from you before twisted springtime
we cleaned the last lime tree of soft leaves i flowered
    in your eye
i also defended you against the nurse's mattress'
    stuffing
look at yourself in the horizon that growls preserved wolf
now i'll show you the psychiatrist's basin
my eye is ground wheat chimney eye
autumn covers the city we share a plate of
    a long sentence
the garden seeks refuge in church
a bad spot for cover i say
as before it was a chick laden with seeds and
    good earth
the invisible one brought the capricorn house to
    cure typhoid
i myself attend to him one sunday in july and iodine
    cotton
death ascends beloved sunflower
like rain with its cardboard flute ring
i come down afterwards from the disaster and am another
the poem bursts now farewell
carnival where loneliness rests and kills
a sharp suffering tucks in its blue face
asphodel of a pale sky rings here
let's make love on this day you said to me you rusted
    key
the badly swept floor was unnecessary
also the sword fish what a killer and the rot
    of innocence
we saw the song very far from a comet i thought:
    it's fate
i saw you who don't free sadness
like the cloud that swallows trash in a corner
    and opens its umbrella
rain isn't abundance or heaped presence
i see a blurred fig tree someone else says farewell

translated by Linda Scheer

122

total union

exactly when this cat has come out to have
     a glass
of brandy in his favorite bar   ranier maria
     rilke
finds you   a dark skinned girl falls in love with him
in a poem she recognizes another sailor   rilke doesn't
     know about it
he'll never know   i think   evil garret:
     metaphysics
of your perpetual salvation   the ussr has expanded
in spain a shark is sharp and what an interesting guy
     this rilke:
he shares his good brandy with an obnoxious cat
in california joe hill sings the blues about trains that
     depart soon
the international proletariat movement was organizing
i'll open a granary
     you'll understand
we need food   rainer maria rilke was born
     in prague
(1875) baptized according to the catholic rite   he may well
     be st. augustine's
cousin   but he's an adorable poet
franz kafka—pity—will die before him
     (one night they cross
paths without paying the least attention)
you're a pastry decorator and clean
     for ford
(the boss mortgages your smile confiscates our
     imagination)
distrito federal october 1968   rainer maria
     rilke has attended
a meeting in *bucareli* lights a cigarette you
     watch him
as you give a final touch to a wedding cake
       the cat rolls over —like poe—
         drunk
       i repeat: rilke is too permissive with him

he'll awaken sleeping in your attic

translated by Linda Scheer

to caroline

how well the dog inserts his poetry how fine
let's watch this now and go to sleep i need it
don't worry soon everything will surely be different
    grace's daughter's name is caroline also from
        monaco
    when she shows her breasts the princess is
        proven
    there's no question about it her friend singer probably noted
    at one time this is cambodia and it's
        inopportune
the city's resisted i'm referring to phnom phen
    it's obvious
but i've seen you love and i've thought it's ours
an american air force b-52 appears
and we leave this plan for a better moment we
hide
    the unexpected had to happen the meeting
        ended when
        the paris adventure club went wild
    with your breasts and everything else hidden caroline and
        we laughed
        i never said this is cambodia i didn't say it
        then
        and i won't say it now
soon this will have changed i predict
you won't go to bed like caroline you'll say this is cambodia
look at the city of phnom phen i begin again
i love you girl we'll be new

translated by Linda Scheer

or volga 1943

end or beginning this defines itself
the red army is checked in stalingrad
hitler was eating raspberry ice cream
a girl walks in an austrian quarter
     looking for her lost dog suddenly
in another house napoleon's portrait was crooked
an empty bus passed making noise at least
     although that's really not at all important
then everything happened as in a cinerama
     movie
     you fell in love with me there was no way out
we wanted the soviet union to triumph doubtless
     and spoke about this in a hospital under the winter
i left you my book of not-recommended instructions and
     the photograph of a crocodile dying of cuteness
i said goodbye to you see you soon love good luck
the vietcong soldiers write poems
     and then kill yankees and find that it's
     better like that
     existence brings results
hitler had finished his double raspberry ice cream
     when they told him about stalingrad
the girl never found her dog
you in the hospital watching the snow it was in
     winter
     i loved you so there's no way out
yankees are dying in vietnam and don't write poetry

translated by Linda Scheer

after everything

breton is mediatating in his library
a volume of illustrated physics is on its side
in no way representing nadja
i'm opposite writing this book
breton sees me and says hello
he closes his manuscript just about finished
i do the same (i come back now)
at that time the snow inserted its mirror
that's when i met him
birds and branches and an abandoned north bridge fell
in the city sparks the snowstorm red chimney
i'm telling you breton life is so important
you probably don't know i'm impertinent
let's forget about it we'll go to this street poetry deserves it
we'll go out for a moment take your jacket breton
you'll need it i agree
life leaps a cat sunken the neighborhood
dawning where this girl puts her ah
it must be convulsive you said it breton
perfect exact unusual instant
let's forget about it we'll finish soon (we've
        finished)
the city is always cold when it dawns

translated by Linda Scheer

sam's blues

i'll say i don't love you
ah yes i'll tell you right now baby
and the happy bogey-men will emerge from their hard holes
and bb king playing as only he knows how
that very sad blues from the northern river
but not everything will be for the best no it wouldn't ever be for the
      best
listen to me carefully please and you won't repent
listen to what happened to me only yesterday
on the bridge with sue ann
oh my god it was a great disillusion:
     the view was solemn
sue ann was near the barbed-wire
     hunting moles for breakfast
look at what i told sue ann then:
     hey girl moles bite you don't know what you're doing
i told her just like that i repeated it to her slowly
     and she replied don't be silly
oh sue ann answered me terribly
     the weather was bad
bad like the appalachian region or the streets of chicago
     as my father has told me and i thought: sue ann doesn't know
     anything
hey pretty baby i won't be able to help you if you're bitten i said
     i was in love with sue ann
i loved her chewing gum during the summer
     and her torn wrinkled dresses
and when i saw her coming over the hill my heart
     began to pound
hey sue ann
remember the walnuts falling endlessly and all the squirrels
hey sue ann i love you and a mole will bite you and i'll feel bad
better stop
we'll taste a jar of peach marmelade
and you'll sew my pants
but sue ann was watching me silently
her clear eyes were like those humid february afternoons
like those anonymous animals you kill when it snows
and i thought: sue ann's pretty and i'll tell her I love you as simply as

that
and we'll travel through the southeastern meadows
and make a big cabin with its smoking chimney
oh what things i thought of sue ann
but look just look at what happened to me
man pretty baby how bad everything turned out
since she couldn't catch a single miserable mole
i was laughing at her and singing like
peter & gordon: hey silly girl
hey silly girl how silly hey silly girl
the mole will eat your *oh* and i'll be left empty-handed
but sue ann wasn't worried
she looked at me with those eyes that would have eaten me before
        and said:
you try there's the mole now
i thought it would be quick and accepted: i began to put my hand
into the damn hole
sue ann said she'd wait under the bridge
what joy oh sue ann sue ann would be under the bridge
that's how i remained for almost an hour till the mole came out
my hands ready to be buried but i thought:
sue ann here's your beloved mole
and i'm so in love with you sue ann understand?
and so like a deer i ran to the bridge to the river
i would tell her: i'm like this mole trapped by you sue ann
and walking on the bridge
i   saw sue ann completely naked what a sight
you don't see a naked girl like sue ann every day
and so i left the mole on the bridge
and quickly took off all my clothes to run after sue ann
who went down to the river
it smelled of humidity again and the day was transparent and cloudy
immensely profound
        and i left the mole right there motionless ocher
and my clothes
but here comes the really unpleasant part:
scarcely had i got rid of my clothes and the mole
        when jim the retard came out of the bushes
also naked
        laughing like a possessed madman humming
"i'll do it again girl"

129

oh great disillusion
i went under the bridge and there was sue ann
and jim the retard naked like god
brought them into the world one on top of the other
like what one mustn't do as the reverend priest says
for it's a bad sin
after seeing that i thought sue ann wouldn't open her eyes
and the afternoon would burst open
i said: it'll be better if i look for my clothes and the mole
well i think i should go i thought and climbed up to the bridge
oh god no clothes no mole everything lost!
i returned home as best i could and didn't come out till early today
to watch the day over the hills
yellow like my heart and the leaves of the trees
hey man sing me that very sad blues from the northern river

translated by Linda Scheer

regarding the tactical need for a prior politization

out of that absolutely horrible orthodox girdle
                she awoke perfect
sexual politics didn't impress her
and so my dear anemic comrades
                i was fine
                listening to an acetate
                (technically speaking)
                of peter paul & mary
                those planetary peaks of wax
and better yet clitorized devil:
                her super-megatonic ass
                the concorde!
and we let politics do the rest
                the content a putsch
                of spirit
it was good i confess it was confessionally good
when her father unexpectedly entered
                that overesteemed repressive
                and called grandpa mamma
                little brother
and what can i say: everything ended!!

that's why she's now quite interested
in sexual politics
that's why

translated by Linda Scheer

MIGUEL FLORES RAMIREZ (1938–), Cuernevaca, Morelos

...studied accounting so he could better understand the national debt inherited when he was accidentally born in Cuernavaca, Morelos. Later, with office-boy persistence, he studied Spanish Literature and, in phonetics class, he lost even the most rudimentary notion of orthographic punctuation. Nonetheless, as a recourse of double entry, he works in literary journalism while permitting himself to write introductions for an anthology which will probably earn him many a dirty look.

His writing is something to do with what a one-eyed jack or cyclops might see: partialities and fragmentations which compel him to experiment —the look as a leit-motif and limitation. His short texts, epigrams and flashes, are where he fails best; when he dares to write long poems, he ruins the long-shot like nobody else.

Totally convinced of his preoccupations, he isn't even sure of his own shadow, and his subject matter dances around like an eye hanging by the nerve. At the risk of repetition, it's fairly certain that everything he says can (and will) be used against him.

An upstream Heraclitean swimmer, he is absolutely sure that he will drown in the undertow along with his fragile, scarce and ideological-cultural load (not to mention ironic smile)—perhaps bitter (and/or) maybe even hopeful.

Books published: Cortos de palabra (1974); Anunciaciones (1974); El ojo de la cerradura (1976); Domingo ya eres lunes (1977)

133

GUERNICA

Alone
the rhombic harlequin fingering his diamonds
the fawn silenced in his double flute
the model in mourning

Also
the bird of prey
franco-ishly devouring testicles
totemic rite of perpetuity

While at times
a goad for the lascivious minotaur
Spaniard of the filled bullring

a soaring *banderilla*
fornicator of the cube

death in the sand
slow dragging of the beast

 a long-lived shout of freedom
before the terrible monster

translated by Linda Scheer

SHORT TAKES

Adherent silence
white mnemonics   bandage

obstacle apt
for propitiating poems

*

(*smoke*)
silence that announces
castles of peace
over ruins

*

Erect in her majesty
the soaring wave
belies the liquid sound that kills her

*

The first time I saw the sea
my eye filled with water

*

(*Graffiti in El Salvador*)
The one-eyed person is prisoner
in the land of the blind

translated by Linda Scheer

One eye is missing
for me to see

Only seeing through the one
I appropriate through lightbeams

Divining how the day
Lucid with integrity
Strolls in corneas of Sunday

Slowly sinking
In unknown clarity
To a rhythm of sipped milk

At nightfall
A thirst for sight is sharpened
As the weekend's
Irreparable injustice

translated by Linda Scheer

ARS POETICA

Either the poem is the estuary
where egocentrism bathes

Or the summer
where a figure vacations

Or the stone
of raising babels over an abyss

Or the risk
of leaving no stone unturned
of the self

translated by Linda Scheer

BREVITY GASPS

brevity gasps
in retina time (wind's mane)

lewd space resounds
duringthe week

it is clearly not Sunday
but there are horses of brandy   or rum
drinks which aren't fattening

the conga's hot rhythm   or bongos
rattles hips of night

        where emptiness brands

was it night
(look at your hoof   or imagine it
riding on a breath at night)

such cold   or heat
blowing onto lips

rhythm foamy temperature
        a being ends   or limps
percussions licking sweat

surely I'm not startled

or it's not true that it was
or only the colt awakening suddenly
or I want to pant into him

then i cut
retina into reins   or rains
the sole eye of the night

the day breaks
into a trot
glans of its scrotum   *translated by Linda Scheer*

EZRA POUND

Long silence   p
                r
                 o
                  l
                   o
                    n
                     g
                      e
                       d
                        l
                         y bent
in the Tower of Pisa
by the bishop-shaped
Cantos

Day of the dead

a a e f i
 w v o a r is beached
from time's aphasia

To the gondola's gliding
Venetian oars grow
towards the t
            ceme
               r
                y of San Michele

Someone nearby is silenced
contemplating the personal effects
which surrounded the poet

translated by Linda Scheer

POETS' DEATH

This is to acknowledge a fragmented insight regarding you
I don't know whether it was a nightmare or dizziness
                    that reminded me at midnight
Because neither memory is with me nor the luck
That someone like you dies in my sleep
It's just that I was crossing a street
Where you were dying as you glanced clearly at the traffic
From a small thread of blood which ran downhill
From the corners of your mouth to your shirt as I passed by
Watching you die speechless for I felt nothing
—Not even has the poet anything to say before death—
Not knowing you or anyone like you
That afternoon I got drunk in *The White Horse* of N.Y.
Where (meanwhile) someone (the other) was writing a poem
Telling how he died when hit by a car
On Sixth Avenue because of his distraction
O'Hara of the New York poets didn't know of you
Or of Dylan Thomas whom they carried from the bar
Only to die in a white-faced hospital
After 8 fast whiskies —a good record— as he said
To go out vertically rejoicing in cirrhosis (more or less)
To find myself drunk where you were dying
This sleeplessness the daguerrotype of a dream
A finger's wound bleeding the lucid nightmare
How to stop the flow of specific signs
The memory of that other poet who died
                    in a cheap hotel
Or Eunice Odio* and her life of broken love

All of this passes as Heraclites' river of which you speak
In a poem tasting of alcohol and blood
I only mention all of this so I won't fall from my bed into the hole
And now each time I cross a street
I look to see if in the divider
There's a dying poet whom I may (or may not) know

*Eunice Odio was a poet who died someplace in Mexico City, alone and unidentified.

                                translated by Linda Scheer

EARTHQUAKE PICTURE

The day before yesterday an earthquake
razed Managua
Yesterday another Guatemala
and still another
Udine Italy

Here we pissed on each other
with earth tremors and stood in line
for the movie

translated by Linda Scheer

Vital spaces
        Mirrors
Recognition daring me
Fixed movements   levitating
I watch as my hair puts itself on
        my shoes smooth themselves out
Seated on chairs in toilets
In the shadow of a light bulb
Recognizing my objectified body
These tics aren't another's
Forming conforming deforming me
Once and again repeated movement
Spaces cohabitable cloisters
Beds shaping me as they sexualize
        a caligraphic stroke
A page for freeing one's arm
In the sketchpad
Facing a mirror
    (Francis Bacon, Metropolitan Museum of Art)

translated by Linda Scheer

TWO IMAGES OF POETS TWO

Dipsomniac — Poet — Vagabond:

One night in New York
All the world's poetry was drunk

One day in Cuernavaca
All the world was drunk in a poem

translated by Linda Scheer

ONE DAY MIRRORS WILL HAVE AGED

One day mirrors will have aged
Glasses will sip ashes from lips
You'll have two dry lilies for eyes
And mine will have died between
lines of absence and remembrance

Then what will become of our desires
Of the wait which weaves a nightshirt
Of the blindness that looks for love
in the afternoon

translated by Linda Scheer

TO TALK A BIT

and what's more
i feel poetry with you
surrendering myself to have you
to propagate the act
of writing desire

i feel vehement passion
from your brightness
in this delirium
the blank page is the road
no words no promises
only the sleep i don't sleep while excited
the soft withdrawal in the vigil
we have no memory   we are the game
each step erases the mark
looking for who knows what
having nothing wanting nothing
only ourselves
the fish's blind eye is the compass
the gazelle breaking loose is the pause
we come to instants fleeting enough to forget
imagination gives rhythm for us to lose
vertigo vertigo's vertigo
adventure to nowhere/of what
the writing is not yet is

you know i'm fed up with being dry
with taking time's pulse
to drink a glass of water
with speaking words
talking is a barbarous custom
i don't desire it alone
i desire it with you i need it
i don't need it in you i free it
i don't free it we chain it up
we don't chain it up we dream it
we don't dream it we live it
we don't live it we die with it
we don't die with it we don't exist with it

we don't exist with it we make it up
we don't make it up we repeat it
we don't repeat it we pervert it
we don't pervert it we destroy it
we don't destroy it it destroys us
it doesn't destroy us it creates us
it doesn't create us it imagines us
it doesn't imagine us it mineralizes us
it doesn't mineralize us it vegetates us
it doesn't vegetate us it animalizes us
it doesn't animalize us it humanizes us
it doesn't humanize us it mythifies us
it doesn't mythify us it mechanizes us
it doesn't mechanize us it enriches us
it doesn't enrich us it impoverishes us
it doesn't impoverish us it dresses us up
it doesn't dress us up it strips us

talking is a barbarous custom

what i've just put down is not my writing
only my desire for writing
not mine but ours
not ours but another's
not another's but others'
not others' but everyone's
not everyone's but no one's
not no one's but nothing's

when i began to write this
i didn't know where i was going or what i wanted
i feel the same except for this desire
to speak silently
to tell you that
and what's more i feel poetry
and the desire to be silent with you

translated by Linda Scheer

FRANCISCO CERVANTES (1938–), Querétaro, Querétaro.

He spent 1977-78 in Portugal studying medieval literature thanks to a grant from the Guggenheim Foundation.

Latin American poetry, unlike Spanish poetry, has very little medieval influence. And for this reason, when a Latin American poet shows a taste for the medieval, it's more than a surprise—it's a true diachronic feast.

Of all the poets included in this anthology, Cervantes is the only one who makes the reminiscence of the Cantar de gesta his coat of arms with a curious affinity for the age of the minstrels.

His poems allude to a tragic sense of life—the heraldic meaning of his expression: solitude and desolation that he sings from his place of exile. His dream leads him to pitch his tent with ghost-names, as a knight in search of his desired recognition as well as the honor bequeathed him by his true identity.

But the poet knows he possesses the fate of the word. He knows that his last moment will be lost in silence; but this means neither victory nor defeat. The poet only speaks of his exile in the word. This is a possible echo of Saint Augustine's mystic invocation, "Death, where is your glory?" in the existential poet's question, "Who is dead, and who is the true survivor?"

Francisco Cervantes lives outside of time in a real and poetic sense which, when strictly speaking, is one and the same. He lives by the ghosts that frame him like a Pessoa and much like Vallejo's sense of human tragedy. The influences of both these battle-worn swords can be found in his poetry, and like both, he accepts his fate as he would accept the challenge of assuming the future history of the verbal diaspora of the knights of the soul.

Books published: Los varones señalados (1972); La materia del tributo (1972)

The chronicle was drawn
in less harmonious language,
but this is not
    my jurisdiction.

translated by Sandro Cohen

I
THE MINSTREL'S DREAM

the minstrel sleeps his death dream
        butterfly oblivion
his pin dream and the memory
          oh the burnt memory of the gods
at times
lays its plucked and fallen wing
on the body's keepsake
        the song is far
and the echoes of culverin arrows
        lance campaigns
        return
ladies in waiting their champion's return
and it could be
that only an armour-bound skeleton
     would be theirs
or a spot of blood stamped on the gauntlet
or death's faded flag
        and it could be
that their eyes were ridden with anger
     for the slain
        and it could be
that the century filled them with ghosts and dragons
the conquest of queens' insanity
the song of hungry or bloated minstrels
        stomachs are the song
and hearts are the boots of old unblemished wine
if you could hear that song
      my love
if you knew that I have come to save our joy
and I am a sudden prisoner of my own pain
and the senile minstrel voices resound
        in my nostalgia
as if I heard the voice that knew not
to hide behind its dream like a squire
we are no longer in the field of battle
I have been defeated
        my flag no longer waves
        corrosion is afoot

dreams will build anxiety's walls
        no more
and the sword will ne'er again be shown
        unsheathed
        or growl in its prison
        my heart
does not venture its dogged voice
and filth is not kept without the dream.

translated by Sandro Cohen

153

vi

The king is dead
and the defiant eyes the conquered corpse
    death
    unveils a smile
displaying his dagger's only tooth
in the king's chest
    he
spoke the words
devised for this solemn moment
and no one saw the lie
for all of the deed were sure
such great gestures
    true or false
    matter little
it was believed sincere
for their fear was such
and a crime is more than a vulgar act
    above all
when it is the same
to spill one's or the other's blood
the killer's or the dead
    the words persist
    the short and fat
almost black knight errant
stares at his speechless king
panting fulfilled
as if he had just taken part
    in a fornication the other knights
turn their backs on the three
who conspired in death
    we may only be stone
    in elegant dress
    only softened stone
wrapped in the most precious gift
making life flow with passion
through all noble and peasant bodies
barely reduced
    to what he was
    and is.

translated by Sandro Cohen

viii

That very same night of darkened fringe
returns to bid farewell
as he shakes the slightly less
           blackened strips
    only he
can see their tentacles
         waving
    only he
knows what happens
to those whom the night wishes to forget
and why he longs for centuries of sleep
    he falls
to dream and hears the crying
something in pain
           outside his tent
someone whispers amid the flags
something that rusts the bone
that dents the arms
and he feels his body spinning
being wrapped in burlap
        crude
        and sweetly painful
he is neither happy nor resigned
he does not protest or give benedictions
he does not scream for his confessor
the keys of the vanquished come
they will find nothing but silence
death overflowing their eyes
     and the pits of their arms
there is no more
no more than armour
        echoing blasphemy
hard and strong
the stout errant valor
and he falls from his bed to earth
      loose dust
      to dust
at last he returns to the earth
and falls from existence

        toward history
        he
who chased nothing but death
dies without knowing he just
        partially dies
with a groan of satisfaction.

translated by Sandro Cohen

STAINED WAS THE GRASS

He descended from his dreams
when dismounted
        and saw his enemy
           still
           and vanquished.
He raised the visor and saw his face.
There was no evil to be found,
not even in his wounds;
and noble were the eyes that returned his gaze—
        perhaps a consolation.

He took his steel,
and in one fell blow
he slashed the fallen enemy in two;
his sword touched earth
and rivers of blood,
the blade was his body's separation.
It was only then that the dead man's eyes
      finally saw their rest.

Stained was the grass
where grazed the champion's horse,
and he himself was on the verge
        of personal extinction.

      Our hero,
      then,
        noble knight,
brother of the sweetest,
      most beautiful order—

      he only wanted to cry.

He saw himself fallen as the slain,
      the slain upon his horse
and he felt the earth expel his body
in a mass of molten lava.

      Who is dead
        and
      who is the true survivor?

translated by Sandro Cohen

THE DEVIL MEMORY

The wind is naked,
Its path still beats
Where I leave this city my bitter skin.
I built no towers—
Not even in the sand...
Nor did this shadow's tremor fall
To the heart of the toll
Where my vacant image roams the streets
And ruins,

The air that divides.

Here is the memory of the Captains,
The devil memory
That carves a crueler vision of another play.

Running through your streets,
I have loved the decay
And your harshness
Born from the mourning stones
Where my pain forged its sword in secrecy.
More than any other,
You are my city.
I've seen my blind face
And a mighty chronicle
That tells where the flower is born,
Prophet of my banished words.

Persecution consecrates you thus.
I announce an unknown valley
Where silence falls after pain.
Our word is one.
I shall remain after you have gone.
And behind this sign I promise your song.
                                        MLV

translated by Sandro Cohen

V

I didn't come for this,
    I swear
    it wasn't for this.

While waiting
      for me
not few candles have rotted.
Did I never reach the promised land
or was this a delay foreseen?

It is truly wise to deny fate
until after its humiliation.

Trust me in spite of all.
I have spoken in good faith
and graciously yield to all
      I cannot decline.

translated by Sandro Cohen

XI

This elegy was found in the alcove
with our life-eaten remains.
We unveil a hole greened by rust
        it raises dust and frames the worm.

All words here are repeated in weakened
                        memory.

translated by Sandro Cohen

PARDONLESS AUTUMN

I want, the Being told his Devil,
To know your lines
          and faces.
The ancient god
took pity on the Being
and gave both touch and sight
somber wisdom,
substantial hours,
          the existence
of mutual examination and struggle.
It was no one's pardonless autumn.
Love was born with its pain
and the bestial caress found a home
in the leaves' broken nerve,
mother of their own consolation.

translated by Sandro Cohen

MARCO ANTONIO CAMPOS (1949–), Mexico City

Campos, who accidentally studied but never practiced law, is currently the editor-in-chief of a literary magazine and is also professor of literature at the Universidad Iberoamericana. Besides poetry, he has cultivated other literary genres: essay, short story, translation and journalism.

By nature a perfectionist, he lives tormented with the idea of man's limitations, which provokes in him a nostalgia for the infinite, for a limitless love. He finds this as he recreates literary themes from antiquity as well as in classical personages who embody the highest human aspirations. And so, when he persists in his use of such unpoetic words as idiot, we react before a semantic vitalization which brings to light the common and "happy" assimilation that we have made of meanings that have become indifferent to us. Then we look back to the myth: the lie that might take us away from the falseness in which we are immersed.

His texts, ablutions in masked waters, adopt a traditional transmission of language but, under the current, a passionate desire for change breaks loose —to be another, to shake us up—and, with camus-nitzschean (in)— security, he does not think twice about moving our conceptual foundations of existence out from under us.

Texts that deal with obsessions: God, death and love are pivotal themes in his poems, unreachable constants that make for an alluvion of sincere hatred-filled blows to the masks that hide us, even to literature itself, which he frequently uses to elaborate his texts.

Books published: Los naipes del perro (1972); Muertos y disfraces (1974); La desaparición de Fabricio Montesco (1977); Una seña en la sepultura (1978)

SEMANTICS

While
a word
flees
bestially,
Form
deals the cards,
gets drunk,
in a
tavern
of
language.
            (1971)

translated by Linda Scheer

A CHAT WITH WALT WHITMAN
AND THE SAME PHANTOM

> *Now for my last—let me look back a moment.*
> Walt Whitman

2

But I didn't even love the fog,
or the deserted climate on some Monday,
or the coffin of my country,
or the patriarch, man's parasite,
or myself, girl,
or myself

4

Walt Whitman awoke in the fog.
While we talked
I fixed my mirror in the tie,
my mouth in words,
a perfect Saturday in sadness
and began to write till I tired.

5

But I had wanted to love God
and the noble word He didn't say.
I would have wanted to love the days
when I was alone,
the tribal joy of old Whitman,
the anguished grandson of my liver,
but one, girl,
still doesn't learn to see one's own skeleton.

(1970)

translated by Linda Scheer

I BEGIN

> *Each of my poems attempts to be a useful tool.*
> (Stockholm, 1971)
>   Pablo Neruda

Pages are worthless.
Poetry changes nothing
but the form of a page, an emotion,
a worn out thought.
But, concretely, my friends, nothing changes.
Concretely, Christians,
it doesn't move a cross to new mountains,
nor irradicate, Germans,
the shame of a time and its crisis,
it doesn't remove, Marxists,
bread from a millionaire's mouth.
Poetry does nothing.
And I write these pages, knowingly.

translated by Linda Scheer

CREATION OF THE POET
OR MISINTERPRETATION OF BLAKE

to José Emilio Pacheco

To transmigrate
he stole imagination's hells,
forbidden to others.
Anguished quadruped
he crawled the routes
with his back torn
by death's whip.
He suffered the laughter of fools.
Parrots of praise.
Stubborn interpreters.
He grabbed his nightmare
at the tip of the word
and spit.
The puddle formed on earth
and at the bottom, paralytic,
the demon was drawn.

translated by Linda Scheer

ELEGY (1)

One, in spite of promises,
can't abandon dreams,
gather them
"look, here are my eyes,
do you remember them?"
And this December has 22 women less one,
it has streets and dead bodies and masks,
and there's a corner, Félix,
where I cry and still remember
when we drank rum and beer
or spoke of unimportant things:
something like your death
which must have worn out with your bones.
This life has changed.
I no longer kill time without using it
but I still invent women and words
as I live this biography-less god.
But one (I told you)
can't abandon dreams,
shout a name and remain as now,
no one to have a drink with.
But enough.
Now only a few remember you
(I've killed you little by little):
perhaps the most brittle vein of your grandmother,
perhaps your aunt hiding in her eyes,
your sisters, or perhaps, some exiled friend.
Now, now that you're more alone than your death
you can think that life
isn't only a journey in friendships,
to be an Asian or European bird,
to drink in the mouths of women,
rather you must swallow everything,
drag yourself on the back of another death
and let pain fill you, and words.

translated by Linda Scheer

MY BROTHERS LEFT LITTLE BY LITTLE

My brothers left little by little,
on their backs they carried the rain, women, the street,
the most fancied gold but not childhood.
What was I doing, meanwhile, what the devil did my pen bring forth?
I began to draw in notebooks
the most beautiful women on earth
who only cried in my verses.
My life was in literature, not in life.
I mistrusted love, friendship, experience;
I lived blindly, among idiots and innocents.
My dream was grass for dogs,
my tenderness a wound-like flame.

For lack of life I've invented it;
For lack of a father I've been the child;
For lack of a child I am the ruin.

translated by Linda Scheer

FLORENCE IN THE WORLD'S HEART

Once again I have come before your walls, country of
mine. It is winter. The hours and the leaves in the
rain fall *and I am another*, you whisper, and write it
on a tree like the wind. It is five o'clock and the
lights in the river are the moons you saw centuries
ago. Dante spoke to me on the bridge over the Arno,
repeated some verses and stopped. There, between the
gray and the dream, a girl said to her sweetheart,
'Suono tua, Giovanni, sono tua." Opposite, in a low
voice, two women fled from my eyes.
    Once again I have come before your walls, country
of mine, and I have listened to my verses and to others,
of yesteryear, when only Tuscan was poetry, and when only
Florence begat poets.
    In the Piazza della Signoria, behind Saint John
and the winged lion, the city did not welcome me.
Frescobaldi and the Cerchi never knew of my visit and
my eyes cried into another Arno. Doubtless I have
grown old. Doubtless the ruins of my bones have lived
on in the ruin of my son. But it is late and the wine
is finished. Battles and life are finished. *Firenze
mia nel cuore*, country of mine, why leave if the river
returns? Only the sea and dreams are eternal; the rest
is of dust and of my eyes, country of mine.

translated by Linda Scheer

WHAT HAS BECOME OF MY FRIENDS?

I can't do anything but write poetry. In a city of
merchants it's tantamount to scorn and fame. I watch as
people around me say my name and tell each other, "He's
not the person he was." No one comes to my house, no
one: from my window I only see the difficult blue of the
horizon. These past few days I've painted a virgin and
her son, oh dear Giotto (the face looks like the beloved's).
How alone I am in the colors, in the dismal clarity of
the chiaroscuro, in autumn's wrinkled leaves.

What has become of my towers and my orchard? And
what has become of my friends? Some went to the wind;
most, most died in my hands; others fled from me as if
leprosy ran through my bones. God, the merciful, in
his blindness, has thrown manure on my roses and has
ground my sun and branches. I can't do anything but
write poetry; my hands break with the shovel and usury
corrupts the city. I won't die in another's war, for
another's gold.

I've grown up in the Florentine meadows and my
father spoke to me of ships.

translated by Linda Scheer

172

EARLY MORNING IN ATHENS

Last night, in the garden of dreams,
I saw you:
            in the ruins and archways
Today, when I arose
I looked out the window,
and in the ruins and archways
there was a spring of
                  birds

translated by Linda Scheer

173

THAT VOICE IN PIREUS

From afar,
it unexpectedly arrived
In Pireus, seated in a row,
women sang
"This is your house," they told you
You opened your eyes wide

That voice, my God,
              was mine

translated by Linda Scheer

ELVA MACIAS (1944—), Tuxtla Gutiérrez, Chiapas

She worked in the Foreign Language Institute in Peking and studied Russian language and literature at Lomonosov University in Moscow. Presently she lives in Chiapas where she is working at the Institute of Fine Arts.

Cultivator of minute forests, she creates images of sparkling fugacity: poems of synthesis characteristic of oriental poetry from which her delicate sensibility clearly is nurtured.

Her emotions and state of mind are transmitted to us in vessels that communicate with nature effortlessly, avoiding any element detrimental to the subtlety and silken tone of her writing. Constantly nostalgic for unavoidable farewells, she transforms time into a landscape that fades away little by little only to appear once again as she seizes the moment. These are aspects peculiar to her early writing, the most resplendent in her work.

Her longer poems have the moderation and delicacy of one who brings to perch the voice of flight: the firefly is at once a butterfly of transparent elytrons that dares to enter painful places, seeking to deposit in the foliage love's pollen as well as certain elements of compassion.

Elva Macías has mystical originality that seeks to unite people with nature, an unusual vocation nowadays.

Books published: Círculo del sueño (1975)

IMAGE

The beach   huge
with no limit
but that which the same image
evokes:
a tepid wave
after breaking the ice
congeals in the air
and endures.

translated by Rochelle Cohen

TODAY

I walk to the orchard
and forget that yesterday
someone cleansed my body
of insects and weeds

translated by Rochelle Cohen

ADONIS

Return to your pedestal,
immerse yourself in chiaroscuro marble
in blue showcase reflections,
as an artificial and gigantic tear
descends at times
from your beloved eyelids.

translated by Rochelle Cohen

THE ROOSTER ON THE BALCONY

A rooster sleeps on the balcony,
my daughter tends him mornings.
And at night,
when the poet sings
of how a flame floating between them
is only a word,
over and over the rooster announces
my treason.

translated by Rochelle Cohen

IRREVERENCE

Some say
that I am a vegetable smile
wrapped in vapor
of earthly virtue.
Just right for forgetfullness and the crops.
Who of the faithful will come with me,
what ray of light?
Sometimes I don't know
what my transplant implies
and maliciously
destroy the prepared ground;
and they look at me incredulously,
arms crossed.

translated by Rochelle Cohen

SOLICITUDE

Days of timid deluge.
I dare you to come out mist,
I dare you to make me wet.
If you destroy my tracks because you won't suffer them
and the sun doesn't smile on my face
and I take care of my coat,
why are feet trampled
on the bus daily?
Where songs of rejected love
sell sometimes for twenty
sometimes for ten cents,
where my elbow brushes the sharpness
of a mourner's useful black umbrella
and my solicitude gives a seat to an old woman
who rewards me with an ecclesiastical look.
My hands sweat from the examples.
I get off before the corner
and walk in misery.
What can I do with these morals?

translated by Rochelle Cohen

II

The butterfly returns
to the calyx.
What a prolonged moment
the course of his flight,
amidst bins of snow,
flowers that temper his fatigue.

translated by Rochelle Cohen

X

Nothing flutters in this green meadow.
Not melancholy for the boldest warrior,
nor the precision of Li Jua
in his slow gymnastics.
His body,
a statuette,
a god without pretentions.
He begins a single movement
covering the moon with his hand,
the moon is a mansion of marble:
his other hand interlocks
hugging the sphere,
white jade in his large nails;
one leg contracts,
a slow inquiry,
his arms langourously
extend with unequal weight
a violent turn from his sole shakes him;
but the rhythm of my complaint doesn't change.

translated by Rochelle Cohen

COLD SPARK

Let silence emerge from you
and from me so many words.
Let a small non-existent brother
move you
or the bud that I lost
in the hospital-white indifference
or the child that doesn't know you.

The frustrated parturients flutter
in a bashful pregnancy
they intimidate me
                    cold white spark

and we descend
trampled sluggishness
little girls
young women
and those of faded maturity
all in uniform
weightless in the worm-eaten belly
and with the decision to be unfaithful mothers
women finally
in another dimension.

translated by Rochelle Cohen

WING OF SUN

My cloistered love
has more littorals
than a shoreline.
My sun
a little shield
an incomparable door
a broken wing.

translated by Rochelle Cohen

THE UNTOUCHABLE LOVE

Light scolds
the untouchable love,
rinsing in its pupils
the ambush,
it becomes wheat
and sleeps in the birds
as in the siesta of pagans
its glory.

translated by Rochelle Cohen

ABSENCE OF THE UNICORN
For Carlos Castañón

My sweet,
where to lean my elbow so I won't wound?
on which side should I lay?
If I watch the windows
they become a conversation,
if the walls hear
let them listen.
I don't manage to see myself.
And here I am
keeping anew
the   tiny objects, the relics,
I don't manage to see myself.
I'm a stubborn weaver
warping the bough, the sun and the lovers.

translated by Rochelle Cohen

ERNESTO TREJO (1950–) Fresnillo, Zacatecas

Trejo presently lives in Mexico City where he works for the government as an economist. He went to college in the United States and acquired a fluency in English which led him to write poems in this "second" language of his. These poems demonstrate a rhythmic dexterity which is remarkable, given the fact that Spanish is his native tongue. In addition to translating his own poetry, he has also translated other American and Mexican poets.

To date, he has published three volumes of poetry, one in English and two in Spanish. His capacity for synthesis in Spanish and the conversational tone he adopts when writing in English are well achieved. We have chosen to include texts written originally in English, as well as three translations by Trejo himself.

With a definite inclination towards naming the commonplace, Trejo exacts mysteries from the most unusual things, taking them from their context to another poetic dimension where they miraculously come to life and dance.

One aspect of his poems is the relativity of identity: the capacity to confuse or give a new image to realities, depending on how light or time presents them, leading him to the conceptual negation of them by means of anecdotal recourses. Then his proposals take flight like birds and pass like the wind; words (birds and wind) that are repeated in his texts, "soaring" words which leave only traces that the reader must discover in the "lost words on a certain page."

Books published: Instrucciones y señales (1977); The Day of Venders (1977); Los nombres propios (1978)

YOUR ROOM

Your room would only be complete
with music and a tired cat,

a phone pleading
and no hand to lift it.

From the window a fence
lined with willows would stretch

and on the wall a map of the city
would peek from behind your back.

Under the table,
a pair of battered boots, your size.

You will hear sycamore leaves
breaking like glass,

a wrist will go to another wrist,
to the murmur crossing your life.

translated by Ernesto Trejo

IN SHORT

Let's say that on the corner there is a man.
That today his son spread his arms
in a dream in which he never woke
and this man saw in his son a bird
but wasn't sure if his wings spread out to fly
or if, being in the air,
he would spiral to his arms.

Let's say that underneath this man
the grass is crowned with thorns,
and on these you can see mosquitoes
swallowing air and the air
is nothing but a background or a synthesis
of the scene; let's say a painter
imagined the whole thing.

Let's say, in short, that there's no painter,
but there is a child, a man, maybe a painter,
and they are in different cities and today
they have gathered in my house, at my table,
and I didn't toy with their fate,
but described something that didn't happen in my poem,
but in a city the name of which I ignore.

translated by Ernesto Trejo

MY TONGUE IS THE TONGUE

Of Italian women
who squeeze eggplants
at market; tongues that can feel
a man like a canker sore,
a jewel.
        Tongue
Of shepherds, dry
like the tongues of their sheep,
circling
the steep embankments
of the river.

translated by Ernesto Trejo

IT'S YOUR NAME AND IT'S ALSO DECEMBER

—after Aridjis

It's your name and it's also December
the last lights of the town blank out
my mouth climbs like the echo of two bells
in a church and stops outside your heart
I watch you fall asleep
and find you
not the hunter but the deer
find you
a patch of flowers
on a terrace facing a winter without end
in other cities men rise
in other dreams cities rise nameless
a brook forks before your fingers
or else the procession of the wind
in your fingers pauses
it's the spaces between stairs
the quiet march of the sun
lying in ambush the words that stop squealing
what skin isn't bare
what fist doesn't pound a wall
it's the snow blowing through every garden
entering every house

THIS IS WHAT HAPPENED

I
This is what happened:
She refused to lean on my shoulder
and it hurt. The sky
was empty and the radio said goodnight.
The mountains around us were teasing.
At times I thought we had been
devoured. At times it seemed
they had vanished.
I fondled the rabbit's foot
on the keychain and felt it tick.
Ahead I saw a tumbleweed
with a thousand tiny eyes.
I saw a porcupine or a possum leap
from behind the wild eyes.
I swerved the car and lost control
of the situation.

II
This is what happened:
You never lost control. We hit
a wild pig before sundown and you said
it was unfortunate and mused on probability.
We stopped.
The sun was sinking behind
and darkness was moving on us kicking
tumbleweeds, blowing sand.
We held hands and drove
into darkness. The radio said goodnight
and I leaned on your shoulder.
You hummed an old song and I fell asleep.
You kept humming so you wouldn't.
You forgot the words and made some up. You
were confident. You knew
I would die that night yet you were confident.
You opened the door and swerved the car
at the curve. There were no animals.
There was only me on the shoulder of the road.
My body a still river, my head a lagoon.

You thought you saw a swallow, a
black swallow, and still you didn't lose
control. The mountain to your left collapsed
and I leaped on you, where I have been ever since,
lodged somewhere between your neck and your shoulder.

THE CLOUD UNFOLDING

But it starts with the picture of my grandfather,
machinegunned in his car, Packard De Luxe, 1923.
A snapshot with poor composition, slightly
out of focus, it holds the forty-three bullets
that pushed for light
& which now find their black spaces and obey
our eyes. His last curses will never leave
that picture, his body will never
leave that car, his blood will forever
cake on the red upholstering
(someone pulled you out of the car, someone else
unfolded a blanket over your face not knowing
that you wanted to see that cloud unfold
over the whole sky
or gather into rain & flood your eyes.
What filled your last seconds were not curses,
but visions of battle, other men dying,
horse counts and where do we go from here?)
My grandfather once stayed up all night
in El Paso, shaved the goatee & in the morning
tapped his heart & felt the fake passport.
Passing for a businessman, he walked six blocks
to the train station, a black mushroom in the fog,
a piece of shit under the sky of El Paso
(a year later Lenin too boarded the train
to his country and left behind the sky of Geneva
that ate his shirts & sucked
his head into a chisel of anger, left
the continent wherein one autumn the Eiffel went up,
a symbol of itself.).
Suddenly it's 1936 and a man who is my father
is in Los Angeles. Outside the newspapers
cheer Justice Done To The Colored In South,
tell the Mexicans to go back home, and speculate if
Roosevelt, the syphilitic Jew, will sell
to the Germans tomorrow at 10:15. My father
is putting two ice cubes in a glass of water
when the phone rings and a voice tells him
that his bar is on fire.

197

When my father arrives at the bar, nine years
of luck *go up in smoke* and someone tells him
it was the Negroes, your brother wouldn't give them
credit. My father nods not knowing why & stands
there for hours following the small cloud from his bar
until the sun silhouettes the city everywhere
and he thinks *this fire is a bad omen*.
Father, for the rest of your life, in Mexico,
you never mentioned the fire, the story of your father,
but spoke of flappers, of Roosevelt, of Chaplin
devoured by a clock on his way to work.

CIPRIANA (1881-1975)

1

There were trains that went in the tunnels
and never came out. The eyes of horses
focused and trotted to their deaths.
The corn slept in the cistern
and was rotted when it woke.

2

An old photo. You stand next to your marigolds
(the flower of death, mother tells me)
and I cling to your skirt. How strange to be 4,
watching the print on your skirt. Behind us
the paint peeled off the wall all morning,
your honeysuckle thirsted for light, your ivy
found a crevice and went in.

3

You never saw the sea or the pelicans
winged like angels. In the end, your visions
were embarrassing; a granddaughter
sleeping with satan; a voice in every corner,
beckoning; your husband, the blind man
lost in prayer, a daddy that would punish.
Your daughters, aging, won't talk about the end.
I do. I take the space in which you lived,
your life, and put it in my pocket, and name you.

TONIGHT THIS HOUSE SPEAKS

Tonight this house speaks
Through the creaking in the cupboards
And the refrigerator's humming.
Believe me, when this house
Shakes under my feet
It isn't because of the train.
There's something in the basement.
I don't know what, I've never been there,
Afraid of the empty room
That leads to it.

(What's the matter with these walls?
An ambulance goes faster
With a dead one inside.)

Tonight I'm a hearing machine.
Coors bottles against Wesson oil
Against wall against floor.
Against basement?
I thank god the water faucets go on at two,
Then I sleep
And the peach trees get their water,
Full of sounds.

E. GIVES A NAME

Later no one knew who named him.
No one cared and the name
blended with his face in the mirror
and the springs under his chair
repeated it over dinner.
He wore it the way you wear a scar
or a mole. He wore it
until it was no more
than a taste in his mouth
that he couldn't wash out.

I nicknamed him. I christened him
worm. Later, it was the link
between us: my guilt, his hate.
He would dream of getting back,
but a nickname never caught,
not even in his head. If he said
snail, if he said *moth* or *spider*
they would become wormy, slimy,
winged, or eight-legged words.
If they were meant for me
they would ring in his head
like the clear bell of his childhood.

Some nights he would dream
of everyone screaming in repentance,
dream the sparrow landing on his finger
and flying off with his name.
He saw the cockroach on its back
kicking and dying like a name,
walked to the window and saw
the darkness stretching like a yawn
and wakened, and awake he went
to the mirror and the name was there,
blended with his face; the name was also
in his throat, a bitter taste
that he couldn't wash out.
The name was all around him:
it was the air
he was breathing to stay alive.

E. AT THE ZOCALO

At the small zocalo,
sipping beer and bored:
sunlight was a fading scribble
in the West, the heat was ascending
like a saint, the empty streets
going nowhere, the signs urging no one,
the droopy leaves like rags.

I'm not sure. Maybe all that silence
spilled out of the church, maybe
the blank sky, suspended,
was the stillness of my life and
that moment was the many afternoons
in the dead center of the wheel.

Then, first on the highest cross,
then on the eaves, on the unused balconies,
on the trees and the telephone lines:
the sparrows and their flapping
filled the little world of the zocalo.
A clouded wing or a black cape
coming finally to rest?

I don't know what followed. Maybe
they kept raining down like stones; maybe
the silence was only inside;
maybe the sparrows were dust in the air,
stars, the black gloves of happiness,
the speech of God and His Seven Dwarves.
Or maybe, you know, they were sparrows,
because hours later when the East ignited
and caught on fire they left again
in silence for the fields
and I stood up and left that bench
to warm my hands, to pour some coffee
over them, to make them come to see
as eyes: not to obey and sit still like hands.

NOTES ON THE TRANSLATORS

Maxine Adler-Pou lived in Mexico eight years. , She has translated one book and various socio-economic and political pieces for government officials, professional groups and newspapers abroad. She now works as a negotiator and international contracts manager.

Rochelle Cohen lives and works and paints in Austin, Texas and translates accidentally.

Sandro Cohen has recently published his first book of poetry. He has also translated articles, poetry and essays for several magazines and literary journals in Mexico City. He was born in New Jersey and currently resides in Mexico City, where he teaches at the Universidad Metropolitana.

Michael Rieman lives in Brooklyn, New York where he teaches high school English. His translations have appeared in *Poetry Now.*

Linda Scheer has translated both Mexican and American prose and poetry. Her translations have appeared in anthologies, magazines, newspapers and literary journals in the United States and Mexico.

Brian Swann has published three books of poems, and four books of fiction. He has also translated a dozen books of poetry, mostly from Italian, with Ruth Feldman. He teaches at The Cooper Union, in New York City.

Ernesto Trejo (see bibliographical notes on the poets).

BIBLIOGRAPHY

Aridjis, Homero: *Antes del reino*, Era, 1963.
——. *Ajedrez/navegaciones*, siglo veintiuno, 1969.
——. *Los espacios azules*, Mortiz, 1969.
——. *Quemar las naves*, Mortiz, 1975.

Becerra, José Carlos: *El otoño recorres las islas*, Editorial Era, Mexico, D.F., 1973.

Campos, Marco Antonio: *Los naipes del perro*, Ediciones Punto de Partida, 1972.
——. *Muertos y disfraces*, Ediciones del Instituto Nacional de Bellas Artes, Mexico, D.F., 1974.
——. *Una seña en la sepultura*, Ediciones del Departamento de Difusión Cultural de la UNAM, 1978.

Cervantes, Francisco: *Los varones señalados*, Libros Escogidos, Mexico, D.F., 1972.
——. *La materia del tributo*, Libros Escogidos, 1972.

Flores Ramírez, Miguel: *Cortos de palabra*, Xilote, Mexico, D.F., 1974.
——. *El ojo de la cerradura*, La Máquina Eléctrica, 1976.
——. *Domingo ya eres lunes*, Ediciones Punto de Partida/Departamento de Difusión Cultural de la UNAM, 1977.

Hernández, Francisco: *Portarretratos*, La Máquina Eléctrica Editorial, Mexico, D.F., 1976.
——. *Cuerpo disperso*, Cuadernos de Estraza, Mexico, D.F., 1978.

Huerta, David: *El jardín de la luz*, UNAM, 1971.
——. *Huellas del civilizado*, La Máquina de Escribir, Mexico, D.F., 1977.
——. *Cuaderno de noviembre*, Era, 1976.

Macías, Elva: *Círculo del sueño*, Bellas Artes, 1975.

Pacheco, José Emilio: *Los elementos de la noche*, Universidad Nacional Autónoma de México, Mexico, D.F., 1963.
——. *El reposo del fuego*, Fondo de Cultura Económica, Mexico, D.F., 1966.
——. *No me preguntes cómo pasa el tiempo*, Editorial Joaquín Mortiz, S.A., Mexico D.F., 1969.
——. *Irás y no volverás*, Fondo de Cultura, 1973.
——. *Islas a la deriva*, siglo veintiuno editores, s.a., 1976
——. *Al margen*, Imaginaria, Paris, France, 1976.
——. *Jardín de niños*, Multiarte, Mexico, D.F., 1978.

Reyes, Jaime: *Isla de raíz amarga, insomne raíz*, Era, 1977.

Sampedro, José de Jesús: *Un (ejemplo) salto de gato pinto*, Mortiz, 1975.

Trejo, Ernesto: *Instrucciones y señales*, La Máquina Eléctrica, 1977.
——. *The Day of Vendors*, Calavera Press, Berkeley, California, 1977.

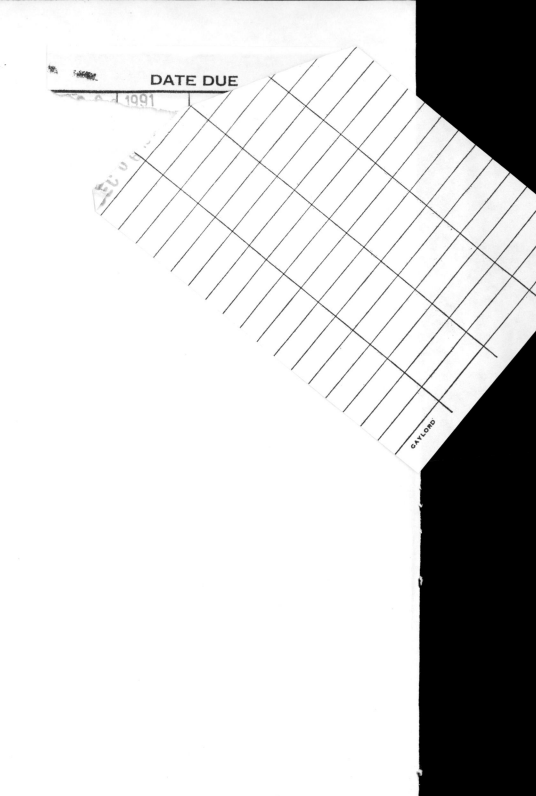

DATE DUE

1991

GAYLORD